ARCHITECTURAL CERAMICS
for the
Studio Potter

ARCHITECTURAL CERAMICS
for the Studio Potter

DESIGNING

BUILDING

INSTALLING

PETER KING

LARK BOOKS
A Division of Sterling Publishing Co., Inc.
New York

This book is dedicated to Xinia Marin.
The book and all within it is my past, Xinia is my future.

Editor: Katherine M. Duncan
Art Director: Kathleen J. Holmes
Text Assistant & Contributor: Linda Blossom
Editorial Assistants: Heather Smith, Catharine Sutherland
Production: Kathleen J. Holmes
Production Assistant: Hannes Charen
Photography (building techniques): Evan Bracken
Photography (installation): Gary Langhammer
Illustrations: Ryan Hudson
Sinks pictured on pages 60-62 by Peter King.

Library of Congress Cataloging-in-Publication Data
King, Peter (Peter W.)
    Architectural ceramics for the studio potter : designing, building,
installing / Peter King. —1st ed.
        p.   cm.
      ISBN: 1-57990-201-4 (pbk.)
            1-57990-085-2 (hbk.)
      1. Pottery craft.   2. Decoration and ornament, Architectural.
      I. Title.
    TT920.K52   1999
738—dc21   99-20196
                                          CIP

10 9 8 7 6 5 4 3 2

Published by Lark Books, a division of
Sterling Publishing Co., Inc.
387 Park Avenue South, New York, N.Y. 10016

© 1999 by Peter King

Distributed in Canada by Sterling Publishing,
c/o Canadian Manda Group, One Atlantic Ave., Suite 105
Toronto, Ontario, Canada M6K 3E7

Distributed in Australia by Capricorn Link (Australia) Pty Ltd.,
P.O. Box 6651, Baulkham Hills, Business Centre NSW 2153, Australia

Distributed in the U.K. by:
Guild of Master Craftsman Publications Ltd.
Castle Place 166 High Street, Lewes, East Sussex, England, BN7 1XU
Tel: (+ 44) 1273 477374 Fax: (+ 44) 1273 478606
Email: pubs@thegmcgroup.com Web: www.gmcpublications.com

If you have questions or comments about this book, please contact:
Lark Books
50 College St.
Asheville, NC 28801
(828) 253-0467

Printed in China by Oceanic Graphic Printing Productions Ltd.
All rights reserved

ISBN 1-57990-201-4 (pbk.)
          1-57990-085-2 (hbk.)

Cover: **PETER KING** (Pensacola, Florida),
Mi Patio, 10½ x 6 ft. (3.2 x 1.8 m), 1997;
unglazed stoneware, handbuilt; Δ5-6.

Title page: **PETER KING** (Pensacola, Florida),
Radio Torri, located at the University of
West Florida, Pensacola, Florida, 12 x 7 ft.
(3.6 x 2.1 m), 1994; glazed stoneware on
steel, Δ6.

CONTENTS

INTRODUCTION

Many of the techniques that you'll read about in this book were learned from other potters and adapted for architectural ceramics; others were developed specifically to overcome the problems of working on an architectural scale. Even if you find the prospect of large-scale ceramic work a little overwhelming, the information in this book will simplify the process for you. For those of you who don't work in clay, this book will intrigue you with its processes and techniques, while broadening your appreciation of the challenge of handbuilt ceramics.

My introduction to clay was a revelation. Although I made an obligatory coil pot in the third grade, I was 21 before I was transfixed by seeing clay thrown on a potter's wheel. At this time, I was in my next to last term at the University of West Florida, completing degrees in philosophy and religious studies with no interest in creating art. A class in aesthetics provided my first intellectual contact with art students. One evening when I caught a ride home with a fellow student named Mark Price, he took a detour to the pottery studio to trim some bowls before we left campus.

I was fascinated with Mark's work on the bowls and told him that it reminded me of shaping wood on a lathe. To me, it looked easier than working in wood. (Now, after 25 years, I know that nothing about making ceramics is easy without spending the time necessary to learn techniques step by step.) Mark asked me if I had ever seen anyone throw a pot, and I admitted that I hadn't.

His demonstration changed the course of my life. When I saw him center, open, and pull up the walls of that first pot, I knew instantly that throwing clay was something I had to learn. I spent my last term of college in the pottery studio practicing day and night in order to unravel the mysteries of throwing intuitively. Anyone who has ever worked on the wheel understands ceramicist Michael Cardew's idea that throwing is something one can learn rapidly and spend the rest of one's life trying to master. This same sensibility applies to every aspect of making ceramics, including architectural ceramics.

My second discovery, the one that eventually led to this book, came shortly after my first. I had been working all night trying to throw a decent bowl using a technique that I had read about in one of Daniel Rhodes's books.

At about 4:00 a.m., after having gone through what seemed like a hundred lumps of clay, I was in the middle of throwing another bowl destined for the slip barrel when I saw a clear image in my mind.

I envisioned an opalescent blue column embellished with the faces of women with long flowing hair. The form spiraled into the darkness above it. Although I was ignorant of the history of architectural ceramics, I was overcome by my realization that scale didn't matter and that architectural components could be made out of clay.

Shortly thereafter, I was consumed with the last few weeks of my studies. I graduated, but quickly found that degrees in philosophy and religious studies weren't going to provide me with a job. Using the skills which had put me through college, I returned to working in carpentry. Later, I realized that the immediate gratification of quickly making something substantial applied to both the speed of framing a house and throwing a pot. My love of making buildings was eventually transferred from wood to clay.

While working for a builder who had great interest in interior detail, I moved from framing houses to creating decorative, detailed trim.

Even though I had no pottery studio at the time, I approached the builder with the idea of creating handmade tile for his houses. He agreed to my proposal, which presented me with the problem of figuring out how to make them! I

knew that prior to the Industrial Revolution, all tiles were made by hand. I began to think of possible production methods.

I set up a small work area in the garage where I was living at the time. Since I had very little money, I built tables and shelves using scrap lumber. To make the tiles, I first slapped out slabs by hand and found that this method was limited. It was almost impossible to get a slab of uniform thickness, and stretching the clay caused eventual cracking and warping. I quickly adapted a more "sophisticated" system of placing the clay between two boards and compressing the clay with a rolling pin.

While this method was adequate for making small numbers of tiles, I eventually purchased my first slab roller so that I could produce more. This machine opened the door to my exploration of architectural ceramics; and, soon thereafter, I produced my first mural. Even though it was small and rudimentary, making it taught me the basics of joining slabs to create a base that could be sec-

tioned when the work was complete. From this point, I was free to embellish the slab with carving, relief, handbuilt forms, or whatever I could dream up with clay.

Once you master the basic techniques that I cover in this book, ordered in a fashion similar to the manner in which I discovered and learned them, you'll also find limitless possibilities for creating and building architectural features in clay.

Peter King

Stonehaus
Pensacola, Florida

From left to right:
PETER KING (Pensacola, Florida), *Mango's*, double-sided entry located in Orange Beach, Alabama, 8 ft. 2 in. x 7 ft. 8 in. x 2 ft. 2 in. (2.4 x 2.3 m x 65 cm), 1996; glazed stoneware; Δ6.
Jujol, 8 ft. 6 in. x 8 ft. (2.5 x 2.4 m), 1995; ceramics on stone; Δ6.
Three Cultures, Two Seasons, located at the University of Costa Rica, San Pedro, Costa Rica, 8 ft. 4 in. x 7 ft. x 6 in. (2.5 x 2.1 m x 15 cm), frieze above door: 21 in. wide (52.5 cm); local red clay; Δ6

THE BEGINNINGS OF ARCHITECTURAL CERAMICS

Human beings have always sought to enrich their visual environment. If a hut or a palace was bare, humans instinctually embellished their spaces with everything from sticks to feathers to gold. The earliest pottery evolved from plain, utilitarian forms to ones that experimented with colored clays and textured surfaces.

The ancient cave paintings of Spain and southern France were planned to encourage a successful hunt or tell a story, but they were also created out of an expressive need. Wall paintings of Egyptian tombs created with hopes of insuring immortality after death were painted with an eye that reflected ancient aesthetics. Greek temples celebrated ancient gods, and Roman edifices bore symbols of governmental power, while enriching the visual surroundings of the people they served. Architecture was embellished with ornamentation to delight the eye and uplift the human spirit.

As humanity shifted from a hunter/gatherer existence to an agrarian life-style, society became more permanent. Buildings created for longevity were decorated with clay ornamentation. What we now call architectural ceramics became a worldwide trend, from the glazed roof tile of oriental buildings to the tiled mosques of the Middle East to the brick edifices of northern Europe.

MASS-PRODUCED ARCHITECTURAL CERAMICS

During the Industrial Revolution of the 19th century, large-scale architectural ornamentation began to be mass-produced with molds, making it possible for semi-skilled laborers to produce exact copies of a design. Instead of using the slow, painstaking process of carving stone, which often involved hand carving the same design over and over by highly skilled artisans, architectural embellishments could be formed in wet clay and cast in plaster. Elements such as window casements, moldings, and frieze panels could be easily and cheaply reproduced. Architectural ceramics became the wave of the future.

The Industrial Revolution created a practical reason for advocating ceramics over stone. Soot emitted from coal-burning factories settled over the newly industrialized cities, attacking and dissolving limestone-faced edifices to the point that some decorative elements were reduced to blackened lumps. Advocates of ceramic buildings argued that they would be impervious to the damage of pollution and more easily cleaned. Social thinkers advocated that colorful, glazed buildings could be spiritually uplifting, in contrast to the gray cityscapes of the day. The

J. PAUL SIRES (Charlotte, North Carolina), *Renovation of the Gateway Building*, Charlotte, North Carolina, 1986. Original tiled building constructed in 1920s. Building was redesigned and tiles were remanufactured. Δ6,
Photo by artist

glazed ceramic city of the future would result in a happy, energetic population ready to move forward into a society of limitless wealth created by the industrial age.

THE BIRTH OF THE SKYSCRAPER

In America, Chicago became an industrial leader during the 19th century, growing so quickly that architects adapted traditional barn building techniques in order to rapidly timber-frame two- and three-story warehouses along newly marked out dirt streets. The city became a sea of wood-framed buildings. During the height of its growth, many of these buildings were destroyed in 1871 by the Great Chicago Fire. As a

consequence of this disaster, which caused 200 million dollars worth of damage, Chicago's leaders drew up a set of building codes that were the most stringent in America. All buildings had to be made as fireproof as possible within the realms of the day's technology. Property values kept rising, and speculators worked to add more floor space to each parcel of land by adding stories. Traditional stone and brick were fireproof but could only be built to a limited height because of the incredible weight.

The reconstruction of Chicago coincided with the development of metal-framed skyscrapers by a loose, informal group of competing architects known as the "Chicago School." By adapting timber-framing techniques using steel I-beam construction, strong yet light buildings could be built to new heights. With added ceramic ornamentation, these new buildings could be made virtually fireproof. Plaster-molded, hollow architectural sections were fastened to the steel superstructure, and the resulting building had the substantial look of stone at a fraction of the weight and cost.

During this era of architectural diversity, buildings were decorated according to the client or architect's tastes. Drawings indicating architectural ornamentation were submitted by architects to architectural ceramics firms that made master molds, cast them, and produced all the components with which to clad the building. Many ceramic-adorned buildings were executed in traditional styles such as Greek Revival, Gothic, and Romanesque.

Progressive architects sought to design ornamentation reflecting

the spiritual needs of the modern world. Foremost among these was Chicago architect Louis Sullivan, whose career peaked during the late 19th century. Sullivan developed an ornamental system reflecting the function of the building that symbolized the synthesis of nature and humanity.

THE SOCIALIST REVOLUTION IN ARCHITECTURE

In Europe, an architectural style was being developed by young architects that challenged those that had come before. Many young Europeans who came of age during and after the Franco-Prussian War sought to build a new society that shed the past and the destruction that it represented. They rejected the traditions of nationalism, religion, class differentiation, and capitalism. The architects in this group scorned much of the existing architecture, characterizing it as self-aggrandizing work of the ruling elite. They viewed architectural ornament as a weighty, fossilized encrustation of the past which should be left behind to build a new utopian future. In their idealistic social consciousness, they saw ornament as a waste of money that would be better spent building worker housing. Austrian architect Adolf Loos summarized this new generation's philosophy with his famous statement: "Ornament is crime." The time called for building architecture for the new socialist man.

In line with this thinking, building materials should be inexpensive and construction simple. Rejecting the past and its illusions of permanency, this brand of architecture sought a

S & W Cafeteria (Asheville, North Carolina), designed by Douglas Ellington, constructed 1929, two-story building with glazed terra-cotta facade.

perpetually new appearance, discarding the idea of reviving older styles. Some architects went as far as to advocate that buildings should be built with ultimate disposability in mind to assist with the process of constantly creating the new. The ideas of these utopian socialists, many of which were involved with Germany's famous Bauhaus School, were given attention by the media, but very few resulting buildings were created.

After the rise of fascism in Europe, many of the better known European architects who had championed socialism fled to the United States. Capitalist corporations were attracted to the designs purported by these architects because of their economic feasibility. A new, sleek glass-and-steel style, known broadly as the International Style, took over many cities; and the architectural ceramics industry dwindled to a point of

producing advertising embellishment for movie theaters, gas stations, and car dealerships in the 1940s and 50s.

ARCHITECTURAL CERAMICS TODAY

Today we are a century beyond the surge of architectural ceramics that happened at the end of the last century. There is a revived interest in ornamentation, but it is doubtful that the architectural ceramics industry will reemerge in the same fashion for economic, social, and cultural reasons.

After the growth of the Industrial Revolution, many people felt that the mass-produced object lacked an essence that can only be embued by the human spirit of its creator. Architectural ceramics now thrive at the studio level because there is always a demand for hand-

made, personalized art forms. Studio architectural ceramics created by artists who design, make, and install one-of-a-kind pieces has the potential to redefine and expand the boundaries of studio clay while impacting architecture as well.

While the philosophical force of the International Style has had little bearing on architecture for some time, its impact has left an indelible mark. Architects no longer learn how to design original ornamentation. This change provides an opportunity for artists to collaborate with architects as they did in the late Middle Ages, when master stone and wood carvers contributed greatly to the overall design of cathedrals and other buildings. Today's challenge for artists and architects is to rekindle this collaborative spirit in the creation of future architecture. Perhaps this book will assist with this process.

ROBERT HARRISON (Helena, Montana), *Gibson Gateway*, site-specific architectural sculpture, Paris Gibson Square Museum of Art, Great Falls, Montana, 1993; 18 x 50 x 25 ft. (5.4 x 15 x 7.5 m); brick clay; mortared brick and tile; mid-range gas reduction firing. Photo by artist

Starting at the upper left continuing clockwise:
JOHN TOKI (Richmond, California), *Blue Currents*, located in Oakland City Hall, Oakland, California,1995; 173 x 1½ x 62 in. (4.4 x 3.8 x 1.6 m); stoneware with inlayed porcelain, oxides, and glaze stains; Δ10. Photo by Scott McCue

PETER KING (Pensacola, Florida),*Manatee Bar*, 1998; glazed stoneware, handbuilt; Δ5-6.

MICHAEL A. FRASCA (Harrodsburg, Kentucky), *The Record*, 1997; 23 x 6 x 5 ft. (6.9 x 1.8 x 1.5 m); stoneware; hand-pressed in plaster molds, carved; 17 pieces in each of 12 books suspended on stainless steel hooks that allow them to expand and contract with weather changes; Δ8. Photo by Jay Bachemin

MICHAEL THORNTON (Albuquerque, New Mexico), *Pillars of Character*, tiled free-standing collonade, Susie Rayos Marmon Elementary School, Albuquerque, New Mexico; collaboration between designer and students;1998; 10 x 50 x 2 ft. (3 x 15 m x 60 cm); stoneware; custom-made molds, slip-cast tiles; Δ6. Photo by artist

Chapter One

TOOLS & EQUIPMENT

I began making rudimentary tiles with virtually no equipment except tables, cutting and smoothing tools, a couple of boards, and my hands. In other words, I found things that would make do during the process of learning.

Don't be daunted by the idea that you have to buy everything to equip your studio right from the start. Experiment and see how much you actually need, and try using materials that you have on hand. If you are a potter, and already have a studio, you'll be equipped with many of the tools that you need.

If you find that you're serious about pursuing architectural ceramics, the first piece of equipment that you'll need to invest in will be a slab roller. Other tools, such as the hydraulic press and draw system, are tools that we've developed at Stonehaus through trial and error. Don't be afraid to come up with your own systems!

PETER KING (Pensacola, Florida), *Palmadoor*, 11 ft. x 5 ft. x 6 in. (3.3 m x 1.5 m x 15 cm); stoneware; Δ6.

Slab Rollers

A *slab roller*, a mechanical roller that produces a clay slab of even thickness, is as important to studio architectural work as a potter's wheel is to most studio potteries. While it's possible to make slabs by hand for architectural work in the beginning, you'll eventually need this piece of equipment to make large, compressed slabs of a uniform thickness that become the base slab as well as handbuilt relief sections of your pieces. Buy one that can produce slabs as large as you can handle in your particular studio situation. If you are working alone, for instance, your needs will be different from those of someone who is working with a partner or team of people. You can choose a hand-operated machine or one that is motorized.

The size of the roller (most vary from 2 to 5 inches in diameter) will determine the ease with which you are able to roll out slabs. Clay will pass more easily through a machine with a large roller because it provides a higher compression ratio than a small roller. To understand this, compare the energy expended in walking up two kinds of roofs: a large roller is akin to walking up a roof with a low pitch while a small roller is like walking up a steep roof.

When gauging the thickness of the clay to feed under the rollers, keep in mind that the clay's thickness shouldn't exceed the radius of the roller being used. On most slab rollers, the thickness of the slab produced is adjusted by raising or lowering the roller with an adjustment knob—allowing you to create an infinite variety of slab thicknesses. Other slab rollers on the market come with

masonite panels that can be added to reduce the thickness of the slab by building up the roller bed. Buy the largest and best roller you can afford, since this piece of equipment will provide the foundation for all of your architectural work.

To roll slabs, slice a block of clay into sections which are 2 to 4 inches thick and position them on the roller's bed. Two identically sized pieces of canvas the same width as the roller, one for the bed and one to cover the clay while it's being rolled, usually come with the machine. (If you need to purchase these canvas pieces, choose 12-ounce duck, a perfect thickness for handling clay produced by a slab roller because it's thick enough to resist wrinkling.)

To prepare the clay for passing under the roller, overlap the slices, and pound them together with your fist or a rubber mallet on the canvas of the bed behind the rollers prior to compressing them. If you're using extruded cylinders of clay, slice a pug in half lengthwise, lay one half on its flat side behind the rollers and the other on its rounded side next to it before pounding the edges together.

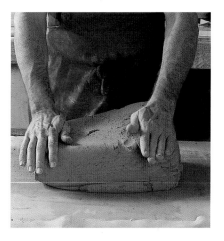

Each slab roller comes with its own system for rolling the clay. Follow the instructions for the brand and model that you choose. In general, most use two pieces of canvas for containing the clay while it is being pressed. Before beginning, check the roller's thickness gauge or measure from the bed to the roller to calculate the height of the roller. Adjust the gauge or add panels (depending upon specifics of

Top to bottom: **PREPARE THE CLAY FOR THE SLAB ROLLER BY SLAMMING IT INTO A WEDGE SHAPE. MAKE SURE THAT THE WEDGE OF CLAY IS WIDE ENOUGH TO MAKE THE DESIRED WIDTH BEFORE ROLLING IT.**

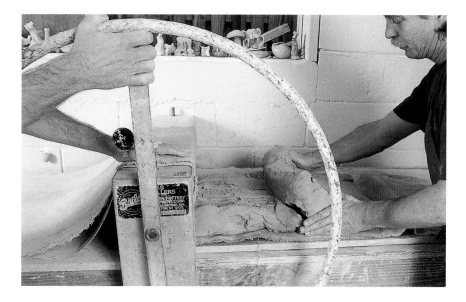

Top to bottom: POUND TOGETHER BLOCKS OF CLAY BEFORE PASSING THEM UNDER THE ROLLER. SET THE ROLLER'S HEIGHT TO MATCH THE THICKNESS THAT YOU WANT, AND ROLL THE CLAY BETWEEN TWO PIECES OF CANVAS. ON THE OTHER SIDE OF THE ROLLER, PULL AWAY THE TOP PIECE OF CANVAS TO REVEAL THE SLAB. LEAVE THE BOTTOM CANVAS ATTACHED FOR TRANSPORTING THE SLAB.

your roller) to produce the slab thickness that you need. Feed sections of clay under the rollers while continuing to join pieces until you make a slab of the size that you need for the work that you're producing.

Make slabs of a size and weight that you can handle in your particular studio situation. Working with a partner will allow you to make and move larger, heavier slabs. To construct the foundation, or base slab, it's best to make a slab that can be easily carried and flipped onto your worktables. After rolling the slab, peel the top piece of canvas off, and use the bottom canvas to transport the clay.

When making sections of architectural pieces, clay scraps will accumulate and you'll have to wedge them back into a usable form on a regular basis. To reblock your scraps immediately, place them in plastic bags and sprinkle water in the bag so that the clay can be used again without too much reworking.

CLAY MIXERS AND PUG MILLS

If you use a lot of clay, consider investing in a *clay mixer* to mix your own clay, since the cost is about half as much as buying premixed clay. You'll be able to make the *clay body* you want, changing the ingredients and moisture content more easily than if you were buying boxed clay or ordering custom clay. You'll also be able to recycle scraps of accumulated clay from projects.

Being able to mix your own clay body is especially helpful in the field of architectural ceramics since you'll use large amounts of highly grogged clay. Clay bodies with a high percentage of coarse material, or *grog*, are often referred to as *open* because the coarse particles leave spaces in the clay that allow moisture to escape. This type of clay tends to dry out faster than others, since the grog absorbs the moisture from the clay. If you purchase a large amount of this type of clay body for use on a project and don't use all of it, it may stiffen considerably before you return to it for another project. If you can mix your own, you can be assured

of always having the consistency that you need for the job you're doing.

Pug mills, or machines that can be purchased from clay suppliers for mixing and sometimes removing the air from clay, are great for recycling scraps of clay back into a usable form. (To make reprocessing faster, dampen scraps before running them through the mill.) You can also buy a machine that is a combination mixer and pug mill to mix large amounts of clay and produce pugs that are easily sliced for pressing into slabs. Either of these machines can eliminate the task of wedging large blocks of clay to remove air and produce a consistent body. No matter what method you choose, remember that clay can always be sliced into pieces that are comfortable to handle and feed into the slab roller.

EXTRUDERS

Clay *extruders* are tools that contain a steel, plastic, wood, or ceramic *die* at the end of a hollow steel chamber that holds

several pounds of soft clay. A plunger attached to an arm at the top of the chamber is pulled down to force the clay through the die, producing its shape, whether round, square, or tubular. Extruders can be used in architectural ceramics to create pieces of clay with shapes and profiles that can be used for all sorts of decorative elements such as columns and moldings. (You can choose between a hand operated extruder and one that operates through pneumatic air compression. A pneumatic extruder with a foot pedal allows your hands to be free to hold the extrusion as it leaves the barrel.)

Similar forms can be made without an extruder by shaping a slab around a piece of pipe or other tubular form, using a draw tool (see pages 18-20) to create a particular profile, or pressing clay into a mold.

TILE PRESS

At Stonehaus, we press tiles from molds using an adapted shop press with a 25-ton capacity. If you want to adapt a shop press, go to a welding shop or metal fabrication shop to have the work done.

Top & bottom: **AT STONEHAUS, WE MIX CLAY IN A VERTICAL SHAFT CUTTING MILL.**

THE CLAY IS EXTRUDED FROM THE BOTTOM OF THE MILL BY THE FORCE OF GRAVITY.

AN ADAPTED HYDRAULIC SHOP PRESS IS USED TO PRESS TILES FROM MOLDS.

The press is adapted in part by adding a top plate made of ¼-inch steel that has a ring on it to fasten it to the press's existing hydraulic cylinder. Two pieces of lightweight L-shaped angle iron are welded to either edge of this steel plate for the purpose of holding a board used for pressing the clay into the mold. Before pressing, a mold full of clay is positioned on a bottom steel plate that sits on the cross-bars of the press.

To press a mold, use the crank to press the top plate and board down onto the clay until it is evenly distributed in the mold. Next, slide the board with the clay and mold attached out of the top plate braces so that the mold can be removed carefully at a worktable.

TABLES

Architectural projects are easier to make with the aid of several tables that can be placed into various configurations. Because architectural projects, such as door surrounds and fireplaces, are built to enclose an opening, tables can be arranged to allow you to work from the inside or outside of this opening. If you're making a project such as a countertop, you'll benefit from being able to adjust the length of your work space in table units to accommodate the many different countertop lengths.

At Stonehaus, we build our own simple tables to accommodate the needs of architectural work (see illustration below). We've found that some of the most useful sizes (and the most efficient use of a 4- by 8-foot sheet of plywood) are 24- by 48-inch and 32- by 48-inch. The 24- by 48-inch tables are the most versatile size and can be clamped together with 4- or 5-inch C-clamps to make work surfaces of any shape or size. If you can put heavy-duty, locking casters on them, it will make constant moving easier.

The sides of the tables are contructed of wooden 2 x 4s and the legs of wooden 4 x 4s. A sealed luan surface is cut to fit the top. (Do not use CDX grade plywood because the surface is too uneven and will warp.) We make the sides flush with the top surface rather than recessed like standard tables. This allows us to clamp our tables together easily and wrap clay slabs over the edges to create door and window returns.

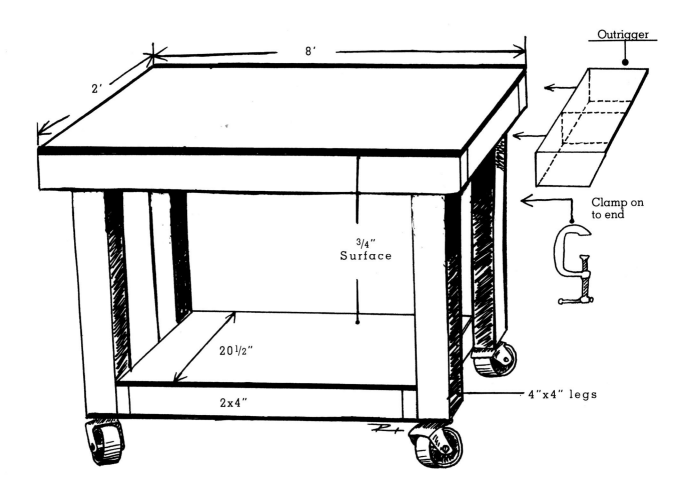

A SOLID WORK TABLE WITH HEAVY-DUTY LOCKING CASTERS IS IMPORTANT FOR BUILDING ARCHI-TECTURAL PIECES. WE DEVELOPED THE MODULAR DESIGN OF THIS TABLE TO WORK FOR A VARIETY OF PROJECTS.

potter's tools, carpenter's tools, and our own adaptations of objects that are made for many uses. For instance, we've found that chopsticks make great tools for drawing in the clay.

The most elemental smoothing tool is a rolling pin, but you can also use a small ink roller or *brayer*. Small hair combs, disposable plastic trowels, or tile scrapers can be used for raking the clay. Sheet rock blades or drywall scrapers work well for leveling larger areas of clay. Detailed smoothing can be done with rubber ceramicist's ribs or a flexible piece of vinyl cut to size.

Build all of your tables to exactly the same height (30 to 33 inches is a standard height that works for most people) so that they'll create an even surface when clamped together. Be sure to cut the plywood cleanly and evenly when making the top surfaces.

with C-clamps. These boards come in the same lengths as the tables (24-, 32-, and 48-inch), making them easy to use.

OUTRIGGERS

You can use a system of *outriggers*, or extensions, to fine tune the dimensions of a work surface made of tables when you need only a few extra inches of work surface. To do this, clamp an additional 6- to 8-inch-wide board reinforced with angle braces to the edge of the table

TOOLS FOR SMOOTHING AND SECTIONING CLAY

The tools that we use for marking, shaping, smoothing, and cutting the clay are a combination of

USE A CHOPSTICK TO SKETCH LINES OF YOUR DESIGN IN THE WET CLAY.

USE C-CLAMPS TO JOIN TABLES OR ADD OUT-RIGGERS TO EXTEND WORK SURFACES FOR BUILDING YOUR PROJECT.

TOOLS FOR SMOOTHING THE CLAY RANGE FROM A SIMPLE ROLLING PIN TO RUBBER CERAMICIST'S RIBS.

CARPENTER'S TOOLS FUNCTION AS WELL FOR MEASURING AND CUTTING CLAY AS THEY DO FOR WOOD.

The frame is made of two 16-gauge pieces of galvanized steel bent at right angles to form vertical planes on which to mount the die, and horizontal planes on which to attach handles (such as metal drawer pulls) for easy manipulation of the tool. The leading edges of the vertical planes are bent outward slightly to prevent them from digging into the clay and worktable. The die, that can be made of galvanized steel, luan plywood, or rigid plastic, is attached to the frame with small

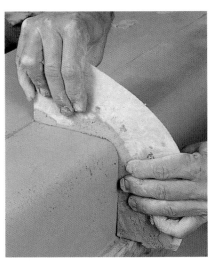

CREATE A ROUNDED CORNER ON THE INSIDE EDGE OF A DOOR SURROUND USING A SIMPLE DRAW CUT TO SIZE TO COMPRESS AND REMOVE CLAY.

We use a variety of carpenter's tools for marking, measuring, and sectioning the clay. To lay out lines on your work surface, use a carpenter's chalk line and a measuring tape. A carpenter's framing square or "speed square" can be used for measuring and trimming the clay. For an easy way to miter clay edges in a consistent line, you can cut out an angled wooden frame and mount it with heavy fishing wire. In the final step of sectioning, a long kitchen knife is a faithful Stonehaus tool for cutting relief sections.

or metal before cutting it out with a razor knife, or a scroll.

For producing larger profiles and quantities of moldings, we created a more substantial draw tool for use at Stonehaus (see illustration page 19). This tool is composed of a frame with handles that can hold interchangeable dies of the same width to create various profiles. Long lengths of clay can be shaped easily and precisely with this tool.

DRAW TOOLS

A *draw tool* is a type of die that is used for shaping clay into various profiles. The profile is transferred to the clay by repeatedly pulling the tool over the clay. This tool is also used to compress and shape areas of clay.

Draw tools for making small profiles such as a rounded edge, or a decorative trim emulating wood molding, are made by tracing the profile onto a flat, square piece of plywood, plastic,

YOU CAN CREATE AN INFINITE VARIETY OF DRAW TOOLS AND TEMPLATES USING 1/8-INCH LUAN PLYWOOD OR SCRAPS OF VINYL SIDING.

INTERCHANGEABLE DIES CAN BE USED IN THE FRAME OF THE DRAW TOOL THAT WE USE AT STONEHAUS.

bolts or thumbscrews. Since clay used for architectural ceramics is normally of a high grog content that makes it gritty like sandpaper, it will tend to wear out the die. You'll find metal dies to be the most durable if planning to use them over a long period of time.

A board made of sealed luan plywood that is resistant to warping is used to move and support the clay slab while it's being shaped into a particular profile, and to guide the draw tool during the process of shaping the clay. (We've found that two pieces of ¾-inch plywood glued together to form a 1½-

inch-thick board work well for this purpose because it won't warp.) Cut the guide board to slightly less than the width of the draw tool to prevent it from binding when moving the tool down its length.

USING THE DRAW TOOL

Place the guide board on a sturdy table with enough room on each side of the board to support the horizontal edges of the draw tool. In order to hold the board in place while the draw tool is being pulled over the clay, screw or nail a tab of wood to the end of the table

that projects above the table surface slightly less than the thickness of the guide board.

Set the die at the height needed to produce the thickness of molding that you want. Determine the thickest part of the molding you'll make by placing the draw tool over the board and measuring the space between the board and the highest part of the die. (For instance, if you're using a simple semi-circular die, the highest point would be the apex of the shape.)

Using this measurement, determine the height of the slab that you need to make. After rolling a slab of this thickness, trim it with a straight edge and needle tool to a width slightly wider than that of the draw tool. Flip the slab onto the draw board, centering it lengthwise. If you must assemble more than one length of slab, score and pound the areas to be joined together on the guide board.

If the profile that you're cutting is thicker than the slab that can

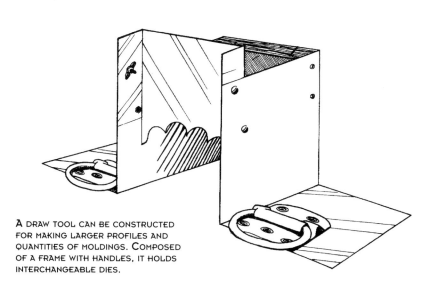

A DRAW TOOL CAN BE CONSTRUCTED FOR MAKING LARGER PROFILES AND QUANTITIES OF MOLDINGS. COMPOSED OF A FRAME WITH HANDLES, IT HOLDS INTERCHANGEABLE DIES.

TO PREPARE FOR USING THE DRAW TOOL, POUND SLABS TOGETHER ON THE DRAW BOARD.

be made with your roller, make another slab to be attached on top by scoring and pounding the two together. (Don't use slip to join these slabs because the slip will cause them to slide apart later from the force of pulling the draw tool.)

Once the slabs are pounded and joined together into one long slab, scrape the joining seams down with a trowel or your fingers so that they are the same level as the rest of the slab. Trim away any excess clay that is hanging over the edge of the board with a needle tool or knife. To lubricate the surface of the clay, thoroughly wet the slab by drizzling water over it with a sponge and bucket. Position the draw tool on the surface of the clay at the end of the guide board opposite the wooden tab affixed to the table

WHEN THE DRAW TOOL REACHES THE END OF ITS PASS IT ACCUMULATES THE EXCESS CLAY.

to hold the board in place. The horizontal edges of the tool won't quite be touching the table yet, because you'll be removing clay during the process of shaping the profile.

Push down slightly on the surface of the clay while pulling the draw tool over the length of the slab. Between passes with the tool, continue to soak the surface with plenty of water to prevent tearing the clay. Should a tear occur, fill the space with soft clay and continue with the next pass. To leave a smooth surface on the clay, wet the surface with a creamy clay slip before making the last couple of passes. If you prefer a rougher, striated clay surface, make the last few passes using little or no water.

Once you're satisfied with the finish of your molding, cut it away from the draw board by sliding a length of cutting wire between the clay and the board and drawing it down the length of the molding. If the molding is to be installed as units, mark them off in intervals by scoring lightly on the surface of the clay with a chopstick or other tool, and cut the sections crosswise with a knife to the desired lengths.

If you plan to use the molding as relief decoration to attach to the base slab of a larger construction, cut it into the largest sections that you can handle. Later, after you've placed the sections closely together on the base slab, you can smooth and fill in the seams so that they don't show. This will allow you to section the whole piece (both base slab and relief) as a whole later.

Before moving sections of molding, you may have to leave them on the guide board overnight or until they are stiff enough to handle. If you have time to wait for them to stiffen on the board, you can continue reusing the

same board by removing the molding sections once they firm up. If you are pressed for time, you may want to make and use additional boards in order to accelerate the process.

SPRAY GUNS

Spray guns, used by ceramicists to spray glaze onto pieces before firing, come in two types: those used with vacuum motors that provide a high volume, low pressure (HVLP) system, and those used with compressors. Spray guns and compressors may be purchased at paint, building supply, and hardware stores. Spray guns for these two systems are not interchangeable.

The HVLP system reduces *overspray* (glaze droplets floating in the air which can be hazardous to breathe). The unit requires continuous, low air pressure supplied by a two-stage vacuum motor. If you plan to spray glaze inside an enclosed space rather than outside, then the HVLP unit is a safer choice, since spray guns that operate with a compressor produce more overspray.

Most spray guns are purchased for spraying paint. When a

ALWAYS WEAR A MASK WHEN SPRAYING GLAZE, SINCE THIS PROCESS ALWAYS PRODUCES A CERTAIN AMOUNT OF HAZARDOUS OVERGLAZE.

spray gun is used for spraying glaze rather than paint, it requires some special care. Look for a gun that has stainless parts to avoid the rusting that can happen as a result of spraying the water-based materials that make up glazes. Spend the extra money to get the best spray gun that you can afford—a cheap one will often do more to aggravate you than it's worth.

When spraying, pay attention to the action of the spray needle and the mechanism that moves it. Fine-tune the settings on the gun and the amount of air flow from the compressor. If necessary, thin your glaze and change the adjustments on your spray gun until you get an adequate spray pattern. If you plan to spray great quantities of glaze, you may need to buy a separate container for the glaze known as a pressure pot. This unit will hold more glaze than the can which mounts under the spray gun.

To keep the gun clean, pass water through it after each use, until there are no visible traces of glaze. Your gun will come with a diagram describing its parts and a wrench for disassembling the spray head. Use this guide to periodically disassemble the spray head and trigger. Clean areas inside the nozzle where glaze has collected.

Spray Booths

Spray booths are enclosed areas used in studios to prevent glaze overspray from escaping into a room and becoming a health hazard to breathe. Since individual sections of an architectural project need to be glazed as a part of the larger piece to maintain glaze continuity, the size of most spray booths made for ceramic glazing is too small. (Since most pre-made booths are configured for spray-

ing upright objects, they are useful for spraying smaller architectural pieces such as sinks and pedestals.)

For larger architectural pieces that must be sprayed inside rather than outside, consider building a spray booth of a size that will fit your needs. Create a spray room around the assembled piece with plastic sheeting draped over a wooden, metal, or PVC pipe frame. If possible, construct a system that allows overspray to escape through a window that is equipped with a fan. Under these conditions, it is essential that you use a good mask or respirator.

Compressors

Air compressors can be useful in architectural work for tasks such as blowing clay dust off a piece before glazing, spraying glaze, and operating pneumatic equipment. The size of a compressor is related to its intended use. For any of these operations, you should have one with a minimum of $1\frac{1}{2}$ horsepower. If you want to operate a pneumatic extruder, you'll need more power.

Before using your compressor, read the manual for operating and maintaining it. Periodically drain its air tank to eliminate condensation and prevent rusting. Change or clean the air filter, and check the oil level on a regular basis.

Kilns

A large *car kiln* or *shuttle kiln*, one that has shelves that slide out on a support, is ideal for architectural work. But it is possible to use smaller gas or electric kilns, if you plan multiple firings of your sectioned pieces.

Establish the size of the work you do within the confines of

AT STONEHAUS, OUR HANDBUILT GAS SHUTTLE KILN IS EQUIPPED WITH SHELVES THAT SLIDE IN AND OUT.

your studio space and kiln capacity. The size of the sections you create will be limited by the size of your kiln and its shelves. If you plan, construct, and section works with care, large architectural work can be made with limited kiln space.

Tile Saw/Angle Grinder

A tile saw can be an important tool for cutting tiles and kiln posts as well as trimming sections of architectural projects. Even though projects are custom built to fit a specific space, it will often take some cutting and grinding to make the sections fit together cleanly at installation. If you don't want to buy one because of the cost, they can be rented for the short period that you need them. Small saws are affordable, but not ideal for architectural ceramics, because of the thickness of many of the pieces. Saws with a blade of 10 inches or larger are much more useful, but rather expensive. If buying a saw, it's best to go ahead and invest in a larger one with a diamond blade—it's worth the investment if you plan to use it regularly.

Chapter Two

BUILDING AND DECORATING TECHNIQUES

I think of architectural ceramics as a combination of carpentry and ceramics. In this chapter, you'll learn how to build three-dimensional forms on top of the base slab and add other forms of relief. If you're a potter, many of these techniques will be familiar to you since most of them are based upon simple handbuilding techniques. If you have experience as a carpenter, you'll find that measuring, cutting, and assembling slabs of clay is similar to building with wood.

CARRIE ANNE PARKS (Riverdale, Michigan), *Secret Garden Tiles*, installation located at Alma College, Alma, Michigan,1997; 35 in. (87.5 cm) high, 96 in. (240 cm) diameter; stoneware; coil-built birdbath, slab-built tiles; Δ04. Photo by artist

MEASURING THE SITE FOR THE PROJECT

Before beginning any site-specific architectural project, it is important to look at the site firsthand. Take measurements, and record them in a drawing. Be sure to account for any existing structural factors that might interfere with the final installation. If you're installing architectural features such as fireplaces, door surrounds, or countertops, be aware of the *substrate*, such as masonite or brick, that you'll be covering with your project. Substrates require various materials for proper installation (see chapter four).

LAYING OUT THE PROJECT

After measuring the space that you'll be covering with the project, add the *shinkage rate* of your clay body to your actual dimensions to determine the wet dimensions of the piece. Most architectural clay bodies shrink about 10 percent due to the grog content. When adding the shrinkage rate, keep in mind that it's better for the finished work to be a little too small than too large. Spreading the sections of the final piece apart when installing, to create bigger joints, is much easier than cutting and trimming the fired piece. Subtracting about one percent from your shrinkage rate will assure you that the fired sections will fit together with no problem.

After calculating the wet dimensions, arrange tables in the configuration of the project. Using the dimensions that you've calculated, draw the boundaries of the piece with chalk on your work surface, and extend the

ARRANGE TABLES INTO A CONFIGURATION THAT SUITS THE NEEDS OF YOUR PROJECT. THIS GROUP IS ARRANGED FOR BUILDING A FIREPLACE SURROUND.

SNAP A LINE WITH A CHALK BOX TO MARK THE STRAIGHT LINES NEEDED FOR MAKING A DOOR SURROUND.

SPREAD GROG OVER THE WORK SURFACE BEFORE LAYING FOUNDATION SLABS.

lines at least a few inches past the outline of your design. You'll be able to trim the base slab according to these marks once you've laid it on the work surface. If you're making straight lines, it's easiest to snap a line with a chalk box.

To keep the clay from sticking to your work surface, spread a thin coat of grog by hand inside the lines on your work surface. The particles make it possible to slide and position slabs and remove sections easily after they've dried. While it's drying, the grog also allows the shrinking clay to move without sticking to the work surface, eliminating the danger of cracking or splitting.

TRANSFERRING A DESIGN

Unless you have a large studio with a high ceiling and a catwalk (which most of us don't), it's almost impossible to view a large-scale piece in its totality while it's under construction. Using an overhead or slide projector to transfer a design to a sheet of paper or plastic allows

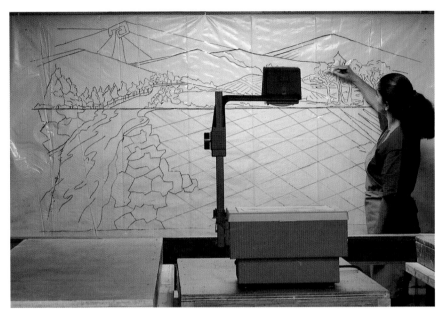

When using either type of projector, adjust the image so that it isn't distorted. Make certain that the projector is perpendicular to the wall. Center the lens on the paper or plastic. Enlarge the dimensions to account for the shrinkage rate of the clay body, and trace the image on the paper or plastic. When you are finished tracing, remove your enlarged drawing from the wall and position it carefully on the base slab that you've laid out on your work surface. Trace the outlines on the clay by bearing down gently with a pencil or chopstick. Remove the plastic and retrace the lines in the clay so that they can be clearly seen.

you to correctly enlarge it and work horizontally on tables rather than laying the piece out on the floor.

By using an overhead projector for transferring a design, you'll be able to draw details on a small transparent sheet of plastic that will then be used to project the image onto a large blank sheet of paper or plastic taped to a wall. (We usually purchase the ends of newspaper rolls from a local newpaper office for this purpose. If you want something more durable, clear polyethylene sheeting from a hardware or building-supply store works well.) With a permanent marker, you can trace the enlarged image while it is projected onto the paper or plastic.

If you don't have access to an overhead projector, you can use a slide projector to project a slide of the drawing that you want to use for your larger template. This method is also good for outlining architectural designs that you might find on old buildings. For instance, slides taken on a trip may result in some great close-up images

of moldings and other architectural features that can inspire your projects.

MAKING THE FOUNDATION SLAB

Architectural ceramic projects begin with the foundation of a base slab of clay onto which other components of the piece are added. The support needed for elements that you are planning to add to the piece is the first determinant for the slab thickness. (We use ½- to 1-inch-thick slabs for most projects at Stonehaus.) For instance, if you're making a fireplace facade with heavy, built-up relief or large, hollow structures, you'll need a 1-inch-thick slab for support. If using light, sprigged decoration without any heavy relief, you can use a thinner base slab.

The thickness of the base slab also influences the aesthetics of the piece. The weight of your piece should be appropriate for its site. A thicker slab with heavier decoration creates a more massive look than a thinner slab with lightweight decoration.

To lay the base slab, you'll probably join several slabs to create the shape that you want. If you're working alone, remember that you can join as many small slabs as you need to make a larger one. To begin, roll out a slab of the thickness and size that you want, then pull off the top canvas. Carry the slab from the roller to the worktable using the bottom piece of canvas as a sling. Hold the canvas with one hand and support the clay with the other hand while flipping it onto the table in a gentle, fluid movement (photo 1). (It isn't necessary to flip a slab quickly with a perfect aim!) Pull the slab into position with the aid of the attached canvas. Once the slab is positioned, peel away the canvas.

Roll out another slab, then flip and position it on the table so that it laps over the previous slab about twice the thickness of it (photo 2). Fuse the seam by pounding it thoroughly with your fists along its entire length (photo 3). Don't use slip when joining the component slabs. Continue joining slabs until the work surface has been covered, leaving the extended lines of your design visible so that you can cut away the excess clay later.

After all the seams have been pounded, scrape and smooth the seams. To scrape the seams, use your fingers followed by a scraper, such as a small trowel, to rake the surface and remove much of the excess clay (photos 4, 5). (To visualize this process, think of a farmer plowing a field.) Use a larger serated scraper, such as a wide-toothed comb, to continue leveling the surface. After all of the excess clay is removed, use a wide metal scraper, such as a drywall speader, to smooth the whole surface (photo 6).

Before trimming the base slab, determine the outline of the piece using the extension lines and a straightedge to trace them on the clay with a blunt tool such as a chopstick. Check these dimensions against those of your original drawing. Next, cut the slab to size with a needle tool, eliminating the excess clay using a long metal straightedge or thin board as a guide. You now have a single slab in the wet dimensions of the piece. Think of this as your blank canvas, primed to receive decoration.

FORMING A RETURN

To give an entry, window, or fireplace a more substantial appearance, a single slab of clay can be wrapped from what will become the outside wall or front into the opening to form a return. To do this, drape the

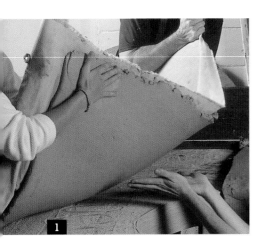

base slab over the edge of the table *(photo 7)*. Add reinforcing coils of soft, moist clay to the corners of the return *(photo 8)*. Smooth and shape the corners by redistributing the clay with a draw tool or die with a profile cut to match the edge of the return *(photo 9)*.

To determine a line along which to trim the clay on the inside of the return, measure from the bottom edge of the supporting

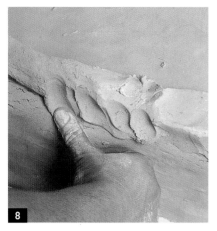

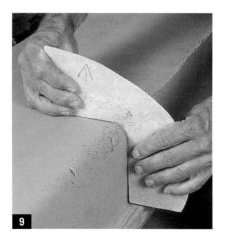

board or table edge upward instead of from the top of the base slab. (If you try to measure from the top of the base slab down, it will be difficult to get a straight line because of the possible unevenness of the slab.) In order to determine this measurement, subtract the desired depth of the return from the depth of the supporting board or table edge. Measuring from the bottom table edge up, make marks in the clay to indicate where you want to cut the clay for the return. Use a level or straightedge to make a straight cut once you've established a line for the inside edge of the return.

BOX BUILDING

Box building refers to constructing geometric, hollow clay forms, such as columns, out of slabs that are supported by internal bracing. Rectangular, square, triangular, or any other straight-sided form can be constructed using this idea. If you're building a box form, allow your clay slabs for building vertical support braces, side walls, and facings to stiffen overnight so that they are easier to handle and won't stretch or distort. (Larger constructions such as this can be done in wet clay, but this takes more effort and can be tricky.)

To build a long rectangular column, the most commonly used box-built form, first determine the outside dimensions of the column (width and height) that you want to build. Add the shrinkage of your clay to determine the wet dimensions of the piece. Determine the depth that you want it to project from the surface and add shrinkage to this measurement.

Mark the outside wet dimensions on your base slab, then score and slip a path that is

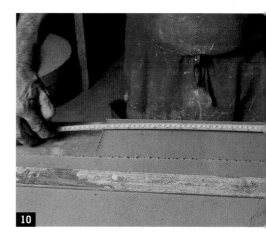

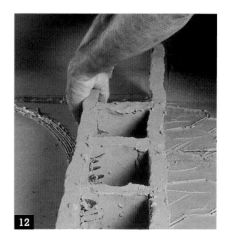

1 inch wide inside these marks. To determine what size side walls to cut out of clay, use the measurement that you've determined for the depth and subtract the thickness of your slab to allow for later placement of the top facing slab. (For example, a column that you want to build 4 inches high from the base slab would end up with 3-inch-high sides faced with a 1-inch-thick capping slab.) Cut rectangular side walls using this measurement and the length that you want the column to be (photo 10). Score and slip the edges of the side walls to be affixed to the base slab, and then stand them up (photo 11). Deeply score, or "sew" together, the seam where the walls join the slab, and then fill them with soft clay.

To make support braces to be placed between the side walls, cut pieces of slab the height of

these walls and the width of the space between them. Beginning at one end of the form, use one brace placed inside the walls to form one end of the column, then position others at roughly 6-inch intervals until you reach the other end of the box, creating a ladder-like configuration (photo 12). Use the last brace to form the other end of the column. "Sew" and fill the seams where the braces join the side walls, and use a pipe or other round hollow form to cut random 1-inch-wide holes in the base slab of each of the chambers between these braces to lighten the piece. Score and slip the top edge of the side walls and braces.

To make the top slab that covers the box, cut a slab reflecting the outside dimensions of the box that you originally drew on the base slab. Score the edges of the top slab, and press them onto the top edges of the side walls and braces (photo 13). After closing the form with this slab, "sew" and fill the seams you've created (photos 14, 15), and finish the box column as you wish. If you plan to cover the box with tiles or other relief, cut the tiles to a size that will allow them to end on a brace.

FRAMING FREE-FORM CONSTRUCTIONS

Constructing free-form or organic shapes follows the same basic technical rules as hollow, rectangular shapes; but you'll be using a much looser approach with less preplanning, allowing the form to develop as you shape the clay. Building these forms is like creating a piece of sculpture—you can add, subtract, and manipulate the clay to your heart's content during the process of making the form. At Stonehaus, many of our pieces are based on free-form construction, and many decisions are made during the process of building that lend the work energy and spontaneity. Don't be afraid to experiment with freehand forms, or you'll miss out on the best part of the experience of making them.

To begin, you may choose to make a thumbnail sketch on paper of the form that you want to create. If you're really shy about shaping freehand, and you want more control, make a clay *maquette*, or scaled-down model, before you begin. To make a maquette, use thin slabs of clay to create a smaller version that includes bracing and facing

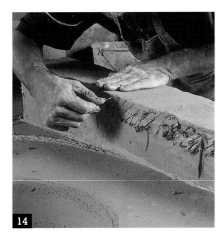

BUILDING FORMS WITH FREE-FORM CONSTRUCTION IS MUCH LIKE CREATING A PIECE OF SCULPTURE.

slabs. After you're satisfied with the form, disassemble the maquette and enlarge the outline of the braces and facing pieces on heavy paper or plastic to be used as templates for the larger piece.

With or without templates, begin by drawing an outline of the form that you want to construct on the base slab with a blunt tool. Cut supporting slabs, or braces, to sizes and shapes that will lend support to the facing slab that will be laid on top of them *(photo 16)*. (They don't have to be exact like they were with the box-built construction.) Remember that the profiles of the braces will determine the three-dimensional shape, including width and height, of your resulting form after you drape them with the facing slab.

Mark where you'll be placing the braces on the base slab, at a distance of no more than 6 inches apart *(photo 17)*. Score and slip the edges of the braces and the area of the base slab onto which you're applying them. After setting them, reinforce them by "sewing" the lower edges to the base slab. Cut holes out of the clay between the chambers with a round hollow pipe to reduce the weight of the overall piece and allow air movement *(photo 18)*.

Cut the facing slab large enough to manipulate it once it's on top of the braces. Now eyeball the shape that you've drawn in the base slab, add extra width to accommodate the height of your braces, and cut your shape out of a slab of clay. (To improve your luck with cutting a slab of the right size, take a loose measurement of the widest part of your form by measuring up and over the widest brace with a tape measure. Begin with this measurement. You can continue to measure other braces with this method to determine the rest of the shape.) Score and slip the facing edges of the top slab, and lay it over the braces *(photo 19)*.

At this point, you still have room for manipulating the shape if you aren't happy with it. You can push and shape the top, facing slab, and allow the shape to take form as you work. If you want to change the size of a brace, lift the slab up and trim or add to it. If you have to join seams to make a large enough slab to face the form, make the seams between the slabs fall on a brace so that you aren't trying to join slabs over a hollow space.

After the facing slab is in place, "sew" and fill the seams where it meets the base slab before smoothing them *(photo 20)*. If the clay is very soft, you probably won't need to use slip at this point. Use soft clay to fill in any sags or dents after the piece has firmed up enough to be reworked without causing it to sag more. Smooth the entire top surface, and finish as you wish with relief or other surface techniques.

BUILDING TUBULAR FORMS

While columns and other relief sections can be box built to create virtually any shape, hollow tubular forms can also be made by draping a clay slab over a

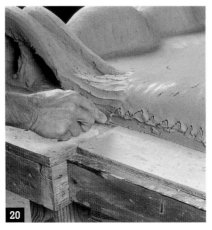

length of pipe. After shaping the rounded form, the pipe is then removed and replaced with one of a smaller diameter for moving it into position on the base slab.

Begin by calculating the diameter of the pipe that you'll need to drape the tubular form, or column, that you wish to build. To do this, decide on the finished, fired outside diameter of the column and add the clay's shrinkage rate to this measurement. Then, to determine the size of pipe to use, deduct twice the thickness of your slab from the outside diameter. This calculation will give you the diameter of the tube or pipe needed for a drape mold—equal to the inside diameter of the column. Any type of round pipe that you choose will work for draping a column, but PVC pipe is one of the best choices because it is lightweight, inexpensive, and comes in a variety of diameters.

If needed, you can adjust the thickness of the slab to achieve slight variations in the outside diameter of your column. However, this approach has limits. Keep in mind that it is easier to drape a thinner slab (such as ⅝ inch) over a smaller diameter pipe (such as 4 inches or smaller). For larger diameter cylinders that are 6 inches or larger, you'll need a more substantial slab that is ¾ to 1 inch thick.

Even though you'll be draping a round form, your best choice for creating the look of a column on a base slab is a U-shaped form rather than a half- or full-round one. Columns that are half-round don't have enough depth and tend to look flat once they're added to the base slab, and full-round columns are difficult to attach to the base slab. U-shaped forms tend to be stronger and are easy to attach to the slab because they have no undercut.

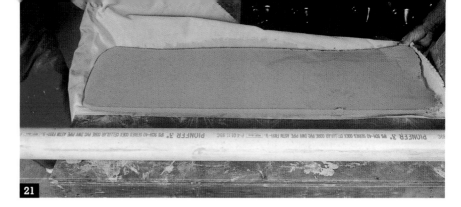

To make this kind of form, you'll drape the tube with clay, allow it to hang down on either side, and trim it into a U-shape.

To begin the process of making a column, determine the location of the column on the base slab. Mark the column's placement with perimeter lines that reflect the outside diameter and the length of the column. It's a good idea to use a square to make certain that your lines are perpendicular to the top edge. From the outside edges of the perimeter lines, come in the width of your draped slab and score a line on which to attach the column later. (To mark the base slab, you can also place the pipe that you plan to use directly on the clay and outline it, creating the inside lines. Then add the width of your slab and score between these lines.) Before proceeding, score the clay and add slip along the inside of these lines where the form will be put into place.

On a separate worktable, position the pipe that you'll use to

drape your form. Block the pipe into place with wads of clay to prevent it from rolling. (photo 21). Take a measurement with a cloth tape measure from the tabletop over the tube and back to the tabletop. Add a few inches to this measurement to determine the width of slab that you need to prepare. After rolling the slab, use the slab roller's canvas to carry it, flip it over, and then drape it onto the pipe. Remove the canvas and gently conform the slab to the tube (photos 22, 23). Trim the bottom edges of the slab to the height that you want for your column *(photo 24)*.

Measure the outside diameter of the wet clay column and subtract ⅛ inch from this measurement. This measurement will be used to determine the size of a draw tool that you'll make to smooth the column later (see pages 18, 19). With a compass set at half this measurement, or the radius of the circle, draw a circle in the middle of a square of wood or plastic that is twice the width of your column's

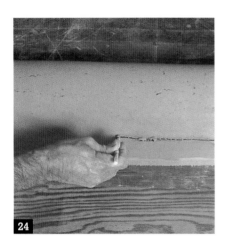

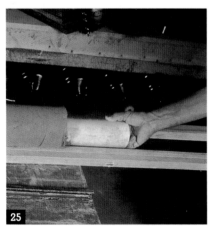

height. (The wood should be large enough to accommodate this hole without flexing excessively.) Extend lines down from the circle to one edge of the square that conform to the height that you intend for your column. You'll now have the outline of a U-shape. Cut this shape out to form your draw tool.

After the clay has stiffened enough that it won't distort, position two narrow boards on either side of the draped tube that are at least as long as the tube and thick enough to prop up the clay edges of the column. Lift the pipe and clay from one end, remove the wads of clay, and slide the boards under the edges of the form to meet the edges of the clay. Gently pull the pipe down by its bottom edge, releasing it from the clay and leaving the column supported *(photo 25)*. Slide the pipe out one end and insert a smaller pipe of the same length or longer *(photo 26)*. Use this pipe to lift the clay and set it in place on the base slab on top of the scored lines you created earlier in the clay. Remove the small pipe by pulling it from the end of the column. Join the column to the base slab by "sewing" the seams with a needle tool and then filling them with soft clay. Scrape and smooth the seam that you've created.

The draw tool that you've created will now be used to smooth

and compress the column and further fuse it to the base slab. To do this, position the draw tool at one end of the column, and pull it over the surface of the clay while pushing down gently. (It's not necessary to use water with this procedure.) Since the draw tool is slightly smaller than the column, it may take more than one pass to compress and smooth the column. However, since the form is hollow, use as few passes as possible so that you won't risk distorting the clay. (After four or five passes, the form may begin to distort.) When the draw tool touches the base slab for the full distance of the column, you've finished this part of the job. Now that the column is fastened and compressed, it can be finished or decorated.

TILES

My first experience with architectural ceramics involved forming tiles by hand prior to buying a slab roller. Making tiles is a good starting point for someone inexperienced in architectural ceramics. Because tiles are small and usually replaceable and interchangeable, using them involves fewer risks than works made of large one-of-a-kind sections.

While I no longer focus on making tiles at Stonehaus, we often find ourselves making tiles to be used as components of larger architectural projects. Handmade tile can be used anywhere that you use commercial tile, such as floors, counters, and walls. You can make conventional square tiles, or cut free-form shapes out of a slab to create keyed tiles. Murals can be created out of pixel-like tiles that fit together to create a large picture.

TILE THICKNESS

Knowing what thickness to roll slabs for your tiles is related to their size. The following rules of thumb will help you decide on an appropriate thickness:

Width of tile	Recommended slab thickness
4 to 6 inches	⅜ inch
6 to 8 inches	½ inch
8 to 10 inches	⅝ inch
11 to 12 inches	¾ inch

Note: Use a thinner slab for tiles that are under 4 inches wide, especially if using them on a vertical surface.

CUTTING TILE

The following three methods for cutting tile are simple and helpful if you're cutting a series of tiles:

1. It's simple to use a framing square and needle tool to cut tiles. Mark off a large square in clay that will be cut into smaller squares to form your tiles.

Beginning at the corner of the framing square, use masking tape or a pencil to mark the width of the tile (with shrinkage percentage added) that you want at intervals along the inside edge of the square. Roll out a slab of a size that will accommodate your square. Place the square on the clay, and mark off the widths of the tiles to form dots that, when connected, will form the left side and top of a large square. To complete the perimeter of the tiles to be cut, flip the square over so that it now completes the right side and bottom of a large square after you've made marks at the tile widths. Use a straightedge to connect the dots both vertically and horizontally, then sketch the perimeter of the square to complete the box. Cut the tiles

along these lines using a straightedge and needle tool.

2. Make a tile template by cutting a thin sheet of luan plywood or heavy plastic to the wet dimensions of the tiles you plan to make. Use the framing square to mark off the top and left side of a large square at right angles on your clay slab. With the square still in place on the clay, use it as a guide for cutting a series of tiles with your template.

3. Make a square panel from ⅛-inch luan a little smaller than the largest slab you can make and flip. Make small cuts along the perimeter of the board at intervals that are the width of your tiles. Lay the board on your slab, and use the notches as guides to mark your clay. Connect the marks vertically and horizontally using a straightedge, and then cut your tiles.

TILES, MOLDING, AND PLATES MAKE UP A WHIMSICAL "MURAL" THAT ADORNS THE SIDE OF STONEHAUS. DESIGNED BY CORBIN MCMULLIN

the surface. These can be pressed into place with a piece of stiff foam rubber.

EMBOSSING, SCRAPING, AND STAMPING

The simplest surface to which you can add texture is the base slab, and you can emboss soft clay with burlap, lace, or any other textured material or object to achieve a complex or subtle surface. To use fabric, lay it on the slab and firmly press it into the clay with a rolling pin before peeling it away. You can also use perforated fabric such as lace as

MAKE A PLASTER CAST, AND USE IT TO PRESS OUT TILES OR MOLDING WHICH CAN BE JOINED TO THE BASE SLAB AS SPRIGGING.

EMBOSSING SOFT CLAY WITH LEAVES

ADD CLAY HANDLES TO STAMPS AND THEY'RE EASY TO USE.

APPLYING RELIEF DECORATION

SPRIGGING

Sprigging is a type of molded clay relief decoration. With this method, highly detailed ornamentation can be produced. Sprigging can be made by making molds of plaster castings of found objects. You can also create original ornamentation by building a relief in moist clay and casting it. Sprigging can be applied as decoration by scoring the section and the area to which it is to be applied, brushing on a small amount of slip, and then joining the section to

STAMPS CAN BE MADE BY PRESSING CLAY OVER THE SURFACE OF OBJECTS TO CAPTURE THEIR IMPRESSION.

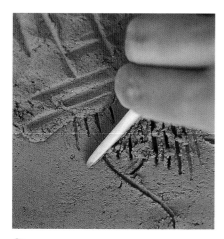

SOFT CLAY TAKES IMPRESSIONS EASILY.

a stencil for slips or glazes after it has been pressed into the clay.

A variety of interesting surface textures can also be created using scrapers, combs, and trowels to mark and score the surface of the clay. Notched trowels make especially interesting background designs. Since clay so readily records impressions, anything can be used as a stamp—a piece of wood, the broken end of a brick, or a stiff brush.

Interesting relief from a small object can be captured by pressing a piece of clay over its surface so that an impression is left in the clay. A clay handle is often added to this stamp, and after it is fired as one piece it can be pressed into another piece of clay to imprint it with the original shape. These stamps can be used like wax letter sealers to fasten the edges of two pieces of overlapped clay, leaving an interesting embossed pattern.

LAYERING AND CUTTING

You can also add relief decoration to your work by pressing on thin slabs of clay that you then shape and carve once you attach them to the base slab.

You can use a template to create this type of decoration. To create a large-scale piece, you can use a projector to enlarge a drawing. After the base slab for your piece has been joined and smoothed, use a template to draw or trace the areas that are to receive relief onto the base slab. The template will be used again to draw the outlines of the shapes on a slab that will be used to make the relief pieces.

To do this, flip the template over, so that the front side of it is lying on the slab of clay that will be added. Trace and then cut out shapes. Score and slip their

backsides before flipping them over into position on the base slab. At this point, you can manipulate the relief to produce folds if you want. "Sew" along the line where the relief decoration meets the base slab with a needle tool. Then roll small coils of clay to fill and reinforce corners so that the pieces won't separate from the slab during firing. You can create higher relief by repeating this process in layers.

If you plan to build relief that will be greater than 2 inches thick, cut holes in the base slab and each subsequent layer until adding the top one. By hollowing out areas of high relief, you'll help insure that the sections don't blow up during firing because they are too thick for moisture to escape. If you plan to make a relief section that is greater than 4 inches thick, it's easier to box-build the form instead (see pages 26, 27). After you've built up the relief, finish the surface with carving, smoothing, or other finishes of your choice.

THIN SLABS OF CLAY CAN BE MANIPULATED BY HAND TO CREATE AREAS OF DECORATIVE RELIEF.

After you make a piece of pottery in wet clay, you're finished with the decision-making process of the piece. You allow the piece to dry before glazing and firing it.

When you create an architectural piece, you still have a crucial step left after building it before you can fire it. You must take the time to carefully map out how you will section the piece so that it all fits back together after it is fired. This step can make or break your final installation, so it's important to take your time and think clearly during this process. Because all of the pieces are keyed together, there are also factors to consider when glazing and firing them. The following section will give you important tips for making sectioning, glazing, and firing architectural projects work to your advantage.

Chapter Three

SECTIONING, DRYING, GLAZING & FIRING

PETER KING (Pensacola, Florida), *Mizner*, 6 x 6 ft. (1.8 x 1.8 m), 1994; glazed stoneware, pressed tile, handbuilt; Δ5-6.

SECTIONING

Immediately after a work has been completed in wet clay, you should begin sectioning it into pieces that can be fired. The work will be easier to section when it is wet, and simpler to rejoin if you make a mistake.

Before beginning, you should consider the overall design of the piece for placement of cuts. Plan to cut sections that are not too large for your kiln to handle. Take into account that the cuts that divide the piece into sections later become the grout lines of the work after it's installed, becoming a major design element in the finished piece. The cuts that you use can enhance the design if they're well placed. If poorly placed, they can create visual distraction, and diminish the overall work. Think through this process thoroughly before beginning.

The sections should be of a size and weight that will be manageable during the steps that follow sectioning. Remember that each section will be handled dozens of times during drying, cleaning, glazing, loading, unloading, and installing. For this reason, try to avoid delicate projections or excessively pointed shapes because of

their tendency to warp and get broken during handling.

To gain an idea of the look of the final piece, draw probable cut lines directly on the clay with a dull pointed tool such as a chopstick. They can be smoothed over later, if you want to change them. (Don't use a needle tool, because the lines might show up after firing.) Avoid odd shapes that will be difficult to fit back together when you install the piece.

When searching for possible cut lines, look for those that you can cut along the edges of a section of the relief—they will practically disappear when the piece is installed. To section hollow relief work with braces inside, plan cuts halfway between the braces (use 6-inch centers for braces). If your braces are spaced not more than a few inches apart, the overhang that is left will be small enough not to sag.

Warping can cause reassembly problems; consequently, don't create shapes that are likely to warp. Avoid cutting long, thin shapes that are curved; they may bend during firing, and pinch the piece that fits inside the curve when you try to fit them back together at installation.

A procedure that can help you to achieve a more tightly fitted finished work is to trim the back edge of each section at a 5° angle toward the back side of the slab so that it tapers inward slightly. Doing this will insure that the pieces fit together closely on the front edge but don't bump on the back edge.

DRYING TILES

Field tiles and low relief tiles can both be dried by stacking and drying them in the sun or on a shelf mounted near a heat source. Use a small board or half brick to lightly press each one into place before adding the next one. Stacking them will prevent them from curling and warping when drying. If you are drying tiles that you can't stack for some reason, such as high relief ones, and you see one begin to curl, place a half brick on the corner to hold it in place until it is dry.

When you are ready to glaze the tiles, gently pull them apart with your hands. In the rare case that one of them sticks to another, use a metal scraper to pry them apart. You can also use this stacking method to dry flat sections of thicker architectural work.

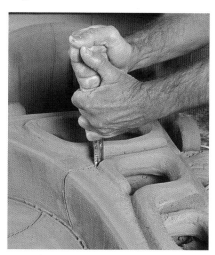

BEFORE SECTIONING A PIECE, PLAN YOUR CUTS BY DRAWING LINES WITH A CHOPSTICK IN THE CLAY.

IF YOUR PIECE IS BUILT WITH BRACES, CUT SECTIONS HALFWAY BETWEEN THE BRACES FOR MORE STABILITY.

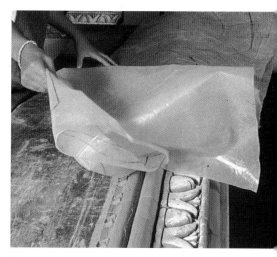

FOR A MORE EVEN DRYING PROCESS, COVER LARGE-SCALE PIECES WITH PLASTIC FOR THE FIRST COUPLE OF DAYS.

DRYING LARGE-SCALE PIECES

Large-scale architectural pieces should be dried slowly over the course of several weeks until they reach the bone-dry greenware stage. Begin by covering them with plastic for the first couple of days. After this period, monitor the drying of your piece by uncovering it during the workday and covering it up again at night. Over a period of several days to two weeks, gradually increase the amount of time that the piece is uncovered until it has dried.

The amount of time that the piece requires to dry depends on the thickness and complexity of the finished piece, as well as the humidity of the air in your studio. Most large-scale architectural projects take from three to six weeks to reach the bone-dry stage, during which the pieces will begin to lighten around the edges. To make certain that the sections have dried throughout, check the back sides of the pieces to see if dark spots have disappeared.

Architectural work should be dried slowly because it is assembled from numerous individual pieces of clay that are likely to have different water contents. Slow drying allows the water to migrate from the wetter to the drier sections of clay, resulting in a more uniform drying process with less warping. About half of the clay's shrinkage (or around five percent of the overall dimensions of the piece) occurs during the drying process. The rest of the shrinkage occurs in firing. Since shrinkage places stress on the clay, you can mitigate these stresses over the course of a long drying period in which evaporation occurs more slowly.

The heavily grogged clay bodies that are used in architectural ceramics allow the water to migrate during drying. Since grog is composed of clay particles that have already been fired, the clay body will lose less volume during drying and firing, helping to reduce overall shrinking and warping.

At Stonehaus, the realities of having to produce commissions on a tight schedule in order to make a living often require that we dry work faster than normal after it has reached the leather-hard stage. Most of the risk of warping has passed at this stage when the clay appears dry around the edges. At this stage, we leave pieces uncovered with air circulating in the studio to speed up the final drying (a process that, under the best of conditions, you'd allow one or two weeks to complete). In such cases, it's even more important to carefully monitor what's happening during the drying process. You can experiment with quick drying by placing pieces near a heater, in the direct sun, or placing them near an active kiln with a fan blowing on them. Under these conditions, leather-hard pieces may dry enough in a day or two to be ready for glazing and firing.

GLAZING

Because a sharp-edged piece of ceramics is more prone to chipping and won't hold glaze well, pieces can be prepared for glazing in the leather-hard or bone-dry stage by rounding their sharp edges and removing burrs left from sectioning.

To prepare your pieces for glazing, lightly sand the edges with a 60-grit piece of sandpaper, a nylon scrubber pad, or a piece of drywall screen (photo 1). (If you sand too heavily, you'll reveal the grog in the clay.) After this is done, remove the clay dust from the surface of the sections to be glazed by wiping them with a damp sponge, brushing them, vacuuming them, or spraying them with air from a compressor (photo 2). If you're not careful to remove all of the dust, the glaze may not adhere to the piece.

All architectural work at Stonehaus is glazed in the bone-dry greenware stage. Even though glaze is water-based and will melt greenware, applying glaze at this stage is made easier because architectural work is much thicker than most pottery. The glaze penetrates the dry clay proportionally less, so the risk of splitting a piece by wetting it is greatly reduced.

After each piece has been sanded and cleaned, it is ready for glazing. Spraying the glaze is

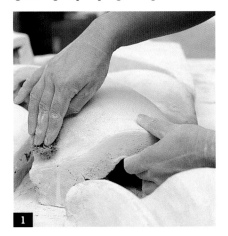

easier and will produce a more uniform surface. In order to spray the glaze on your sections, you'll need to first reassemble your piece, leaving a small, ¼-inch space between each section. (If the pieces are placed too tightly together, the glaze will span the seam. When the pieces are moved for loading into the kiln, the glaze will break away from these edges. If this does occur, touch up the edges with a brush.) Separating the pieces also allows you to cover the edges of them with glaze (photo 3), so that when the piece is installed, there won't be unglazed clay showing along the grout joints.

If you're using several glazes when spraying a piece, you can mask areas to protect one area of glaze while spraying another. One method is to first use a brush or ear syringe to apply sections of glaze, then,

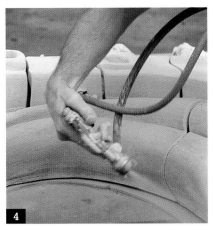

after those sections have dried, paint ceramic wax on them before spraying the other areas. You can also paint latex rubber on the areas that you want to protect while spray glazing larger sections.

A masking technique that we like to use at Stonehaus uses thin slabs of clay (about ⅛ inch thick) placed over areas that we want to protect while we spray the larger areas. After spraying, peel the clay masks off and discard them so that they won't accidentally be remixed with your clay body.

In order to create a consistent glaze surface on your piece, you must spray it on with a uniform thickness. Begin by mixing glaze that is the consistency of cream. Then, holding the spray gun 8 to 12 inches from the surface, apply the glaze with a series of smooth passes (photo 4). To accomplish this, depress the trigger of the gun at the same moment you begin moving your hand across the surface, and release the trigger at the end of each pass. The rate at which you move your hand will determine the amount of glaze deposited on the surface of the clay. Read the spray gun manual to find out how to adjust the amount of glaze and air coming out of the nozzle. You may need to make adjustments to your spray gun and thin the glaze in order to get a smooth spray. Before spraying your piece, test the sprayer on newspaper or another surface to find the result that you want.

Once the glaze is dry, disassemble the work enough to check the back side of each section for glaze drips or overspray. Drips can fuse onto the kiln shelf and cause sections to split during cooling, because they won't be able to contract and move

freely across the surface of the shelf. To avoid this, scrape any excess glaze off with a needle tool or scraper before loading sections onto the kiln shelf.

FIRING

LOADING THE KILN

Unless you have the luxury of a car kiln and a crane, section your work into pieces of a size that you can easily lift and fit onto your kiln's shelves. To efficiently load the kiln, you should be able to place kiln posts around all but the few pieces that can be placed on the top shelf. To maximize space, section architectural pieces into a wide variety of shapes and sizes. You'll be able to place large pieces on the shelves first and then position small ones around them. Try to place pieces of similar height together on the same shelf. A section can be allowed to project past the shelf's edge, but it shouldn't do so more than three times its thickness. (In other words, depending on its shape, a 1-inch-thick section can be allowed to project 3 inches past the edge of the shelf.) The weight of large pieces should be distributed over the surface of the shelf so that the point load, or amount of downward force, is distributed across the shelf.

The kiln load's weight should be uniformly distributed. If you pack a gas kiln tightly in one area and leave it open in another, it is likely that your firing will be uneven (this is not as much of an issue if you're using an electric kiln, which tends to fire more uniformly). If you load a gas kiln with an architectural piece that is spread throughout the kiln, the placement and location of the individual pieces in the kiln become paramount, because the final work must read as a single piece when it is reassembled. It helps to load the kiln with the relationship of the individual sections in mind, placing pieces next to one another that will be adjacent in the installation. By doing this, the pieces will have a chance to fire at a similar temperature if there are variations in the kiln.

Firebricks, or bricks made especially to handle heat load, make convenient, inexpensive, and durable kiln stilts for architectural pieces. These bricks, which can be ordered from refractory brick suppliers are heat-graded and come printed with a name indicating the PCE grade (pyrometric cone equivalent). Because of the heavier weight of architectural sections, commercial shelf posts are sometimes not strong enough, but a high-temperature firebrick can withstand a considerable compressive load. Using standard-sized firebricks as stilts, it is possible to obtain various heights by standing bricks up vertically, turning them edgewise, or laying them flat. You can also cut firebricks to size using a tile saw, or break them with a cold chisel and a hammer. Using brick pieces and kiln shelf scraps for fine-tuning the height of each shelf makes it possible to achieve a compact kiln load.

When possible, use three-point posting rather than four-point because the stresses are distributed diagonally across the shelf, reducing the risk of shelves warping. At times it is necessary to place stilts at each corner of the shelf to accommodate certain shapes. To prevent the shelf from rocking, place soft wads of clay rolled in grog or alumina on top of each stilt and gently lower the kiln shelf into position.

Firing Guidelines

A few guidelines for architectural firings differ from those for standard pottery or tile firings. First, be certain to put grog or sand under large flat pieces to allow the pieces to move as they shrink. Keep the grog away from the shelf edges so that it doesn't fall down onto the work below.

In general, fire architectural work slowly. A *pyrometer* is recommended to monitor the rate of firing. In the beginning, fire a fairly long or overnight *candle period* with the pieces drying around 100° C (212° F) to drive off the atmospheric water. If you're firing a gas kiln, leave your damper and spyholes wide open to allow the escape of moisture during this period. In the case of an electric kiln, leave the lid and the spyholes open.

Fire up the kiln slowly, beginning with a rate of no more than 75° C (153° F) per hour. If using an electric kiln, leave the lid cracked slightly until the temperature reaches about 500° C (932° F). Adjust the rate based on the thickness of your pieces. Thicker pieces will need to be fired more slowly because water has to migrate further to escape during the firing process. If thick pieces are fired too quickly, excessive steam can build up and cause them to blow apart.

Soaking and Cooling

Architectural pieces need to be fired slowly and evenly, and a total firing can take from 18 to 40 hours in a gas kiln and 24 hours in an electric kiln. To assure even heat at the end of your firing, hold the temperature steady at the end for a soak, giving cooler sections time to catch up. Allow time for a slow and even cooling of the kiln as well.

Unloading

When unloading the kiln, carefully remove sections one at a time. Once a shelf is empty, gently lift it out and away from the next one. Watch out for kiln posts stuck to the bottom of the shelves that could fall on the work below as you move the shelf. Losing a piece of a multi-part project can be a nightmare, so be especially careful at this final stage of the firing process.

After the work is removed from the kiln, review each section for any glaze that may have run down an edge during firing, since glaze drips can interfere with a good fit between the various sections upon installation. Remove any drips with a small side grinder carrying a dry-cutting diamond blade; then test-fit the adjacent sections. After cleaning up the pieces, reassemble the whole piece on tables or on the floor to make certain that all sections fit.

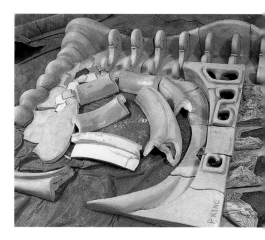

Clay Bodies and Freeze Thaw

Because many architectural ceramic projects are installed outside, it is important to understand how this can impact your work. Projects exposed to freezing conditions must be frost proof, or impervious to the effects of freezing water that can expand and break apart the clay, ultimately causing the surface to flake off. This reaction is called *freeze thaw spalling*.

To prevent this, both the clay body that you use and the temperature to which it is fired are key factors. A clay body for outside use must have particles that have been fused by high kiln heat into a state that is vitreous enough to withstand the pressure of freezing water. (If a clay body is not fired hot enough it will remain absorptive, because the clay particles aren't sufficiently melted and fused together.) A highly grogged clay body that is fired correctly will be porous, but not excessively absorptive.

If you choose or mix a clay with about 30 percent fireclay and 30 percent grog, and fire it to at least cone 5, it will be resistant to warping and cracking while you're making the piece, as well as being able to withstand the rigors of freezing and thawing after it is installed outside.

To mix the clay body that we use at Stonehaus, we mine a local, fine-bodied plastic clay that is composed largely of secondary kaolin, or kaolin that has been deposited by the weathering of feldspathic rock. The recipe is composed of the following:

Stonehaus Clay Body (Cone 6)

COMPONENTS	PERCENT
Local clay	35
Fireclay	29
20-mesh grog	29
Feldspar	7

We add feldspar to our clay body to melt the excess free silica that occurs in our locally mined clay. (This may not be necessary in the substitute version of the recipe that you'll find below.) If you add 10 percent feldspar to the recipe, it will lower the maturation point of a cone 10 clay body to the cone 5 to 6 range. This will enable you to fire such a clay formula to that range and still be able to use it in outdoor settings.

This recipe is a close substitute for the one above:

Stonehaus Recipe Substitute (Cone 6)

COMPONENTS	PERCENT
Throwing clay	33
Fireclay	33
20-mesh grog	33

The following recipes also work well for architectural ceramics:

Terri Vance's Clay Body Recipe (Cone 6)

COMPONENTS	PERCENT
Fireclay	60
Ball clay	15
Custer Spar	2
Wollastonite	3
Grog (20-28 mesh)	20
Flint 325	5

Linda Blossom's Clay Body Recipe (Cone 6)

COMPONENTS	PERCENT
Hawthorn Bond	35
OM4 Ball Clay	20
Newman Red	15
Fine grog (48 mesh)	20
Silica	10

If you would like to try paper clay, you can use the following adapted version of the previous recipe. This clay has a high capacity for water absorption and is remarkably strong in the wet and greenware state.

Paper Clay (Cone 6)

COMPONENTS	PERCENT
Hawthorn Bond	45
OM4 Ball Clay	10
Newman Red	25
Silica	10
Fine grog (48 mesh)	10

Add:

Paper pulp 25-30% by volume

To make paper pulp, add paper to hot water in a bucket, and let it sit for a few hours to dissolve. Then blend the two components with a mixer blade. Pour the pulp into the clay mixer, and follow with the dry clay ingredients. Mix until the paper is barely visible. When you pull the clay apart and hold it to light, you should see small paper fibers.

Chapter Four

INSTALLATION

Most potters are inexperienced with the techniques and materials of installing architectural ceramics. Instead of being daunted by this process, think of it as another form of handbuilding that is a natural extension of the work required to make the piece. Seeing the piece come together as a whole in the final stage can be one of the most exciting and satisfying points in the process of making it.

JOHN TOKI (Richmond, California), *O*, sited at Oakland Museum of California, Oakland, California, 1993; 20 x 24 x 96 in. (50 x 60 cm x 2.4 m); stoneware and porcelain clays with oxide and glaze stain pigments; slab-constructed, made in sections; Δ10; each ceramic section connected to interior steel pipe armature with tie-rods, pipe bolted to steel base for reinforcement against earthquake activity. Photo by Scott McCue

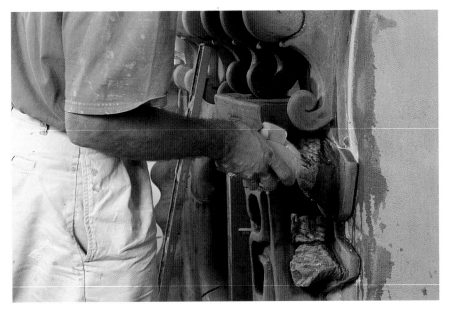

A FIREPLACE INSTALLATION NEARING COMPLETION

The method of installation chosen for a given job will depend on two factors: the type of substrate you'll be setting the sections onto, and whether you want to install the piece permanently or in a way that allows the piece to be moved. You can combine any of the various methods of installation discussed below, depending on your needs.

In most construction, you're apt to find one of several surfaces that require different preparation: drywall, wood (plywood, plank, tongue-in-groove), masonry (block, poured concrete, brick, or stone), or elastic membrane surfaces. The following section will tell you how to prepare for installing on these substrates.

After the pieces of your project are fired, lay out all the parts to see if they're present and fit together. Double-check the dimensions of the piece to make certain that it will match the site that you're installing. Check each section for glaze drips, and remove them by chipping them away with a hammer. Delicate sections may require a grinder or tile saw.

If you want, you can make the installation easier later by making a drawing of the sections and assigning numbers to the parts on paper as well as on the back of the ceramic sections. Take this map to the installation site, and you won't have to waste time contemplating the position of the next piece in your jigsaw puzzle.

After this preinstallation check is complete, carefully wrap and box the pieces if you're transporting them to another site. Don't take chances on any section getting broken. Wrap them with plenty of padding—scraps of carpet padding work well and can be obtained free from an installer.

SURFACE PREPARATION

By the time you get to this stage, you should be very familiar with the site where you'll be mounting the project. You'll need to take all the tools and adhesives with you that you need to complete the installation. Different surfaces require different application techniques, so be thoroughly educated about what you need to do for your particular installation before attempting it. The

KEY TOGETHER THE PIECES OF YOUR PROJECT ON THE FLOOR BEFORE INSTALLING IT.

NUMBER YOUR PIECES ON THE BACK TO MAKE INSTALLATION EASIER.

following section will help you make intelligent choices.

Before the piece is unboxed at the site, the surface onto which you'll be setting the pieces needs to be prepped. If it is an older masonry surface such as concrete block, brick, or stucco, it is essential to remove all dirt, dust, oil, and organic debris. If the surface isn't excessively dirty, wear latex gloves and scrub the surface with a solution of bleach and water. If the surface is extremely soiled, thoroughly scrub the surface with a solution of muratic acid applied with a brush made for this use. This solvent is especially effective for cleaning cement-based surfaces, because it reacts chemically with the surface and burns off the skin of the old surface.

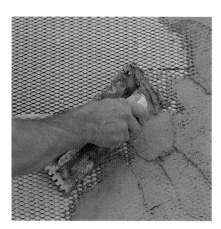

FOR EXTRA INSURANCE, COAT MASONRY SURFACES WITH A LAYER OF BONDING ADHESIVE BEFORE ADDING THE SETTING COMPOUND.

TO STRENGTHEN THE SUBSTRATE, ATTACH AN INTERFACE OF EXPANDED WIRE LATH TO IT BEFORE APPLYING MORTAR.

The acid can burn your skin, so wear a pair of latex gloves and clothing that covers exposed skin. Wear a respirator to protect yourself from harmful fumes. After scrubbing the surface with acid, rinse it well with water or the acid will continue to react.

Old-painted surfaces may require sandblasting to clean them. Unless you have access to sandblasting equipment and know how to use it, delegate this work to a professional. If you're installing onto a fresh or new masonry surface, it will probably only need to be dusted with a dry brush in order to be ready.

In our routine at Stonehaus for installing on a masonry surface, we normally coat it with a layer of latex or acrylic bonding adhesive. Doing this provides extra insurance of a good bond at the interface of the existing masonry and the setting compound. Apply this adhesive with a paint roller, or brush onto the installation surface as if you were applying latex paint.

Prepping a drywall surface entails a different procedure than masonry. Although a great deal of commercial tile is set directly onto drywall, the weight of architectural sections requires a strengthened substrate. For this reason, we fasten

TO PROTECT COUNTERTOPS FROM WATER INTRUSION, PUT DOWN A LAYER OF FELT BETWEEN THE SUBSTRATE AND THE EXPANDED WIRE LATH.

a sheet of expanded wire lath to the drywall studs using screws or nails to provide another layer to hold the pieces in place.

After adding this wire, the drywall will become no more than a backing for the wire. (You can also use tile-backer board, made of concrete and fiberglass mesh, in place of the wire.)

To make an expanded wire interface, trim the wire with wire-cutters to the shape of the piece you're installing. Take care to ensure that it is well within the perimeter dimensions of the piece, so that it won't show after you've installed the sections. Once the wire is firmly fastened to the drywall studs, flatten any bulges in it by stapling it to the drywall.

When working over expanded wire, tile setters usually apply a mortar bed or "brown coat" to the wire, which is allowed to set for a day, before cementing tile to the surface. The process is different when installing fairly large sections, because of their thickness, size, and irregular shape. At Stonehaus, we usually forgo a preliminary mortar bed. Instead, we set our work directly into a single layer of thinset (described on page 43) that has been thoroughly embedded into the expanded wire.

When installing ceramic countertop sections (usually mounted on plywood), it is important to lay down a vapor barrier between the wooden top and the expanded wire to protect the wood from water intrusion. To do this, use a sheet of 4 to 6 mm plastic or 30-pound organic felt to cover the countertop surface and at least 3 inches of the backsplash area before stapling wire over it. You can also put a layer of cement backerboard directly on the plywood as a water-resistant interface.

SETTING

Thinset has distinct advantages over conventional mortar for setting architectural ceramics. First, it has a much higher viscosity, which makes vertical application easier and allows pieces to adhere to the wall without falling off. Thinset also has a much slower setting time, which makes it possible to slide sections around without breaking the bond at the interface between the materials. This is especially helpful with custom-fitted pieces, because even though a panel may have been cut from a single piece of clay, it rarely fits back together perfectly, and it's often necessary to make adjustments during setting.

Sometimes referred to as bonding mortar, thinset was first developed during the 1960s and has been modified over time with the addition of polymer additives to increase strength and adhesion. Present-day versions of this compound would probably seem like magic to tile setters of the previous era.

Various types of thinset are designed for different applications. They range from a basic unmodified mortar without polymer additives designed for installing tiles on a horizontal masonry substrate, to highly polymer-modified mortar designed for a wide range of applications including vertical installations. (If you wish to increase the strength of an unmodified mortar, this mortar can be purchased separately and mixed with liquid additive instead of water.) Thinset compounds range in price, so it's important to select it based on how it will be used. If you feel uncertain about which to buy, go with a higher grade of thinset. For most Stonehaus installa-

tions, we use multi-purpose thinset and latex admixture.

Before mixing and applying thinset, unbox the sections of your piece and reassemble them near the installation site on the floor. Doing this makes picking up and setting the pieces into place much easier within the limited time that thinset is workable before it becomes unusable. If setting a vertical installation, such as a fireplace, plan to work from the bottom of the piece to the top.

Once the piece is laid out, mix a batch of thinset in a bucket as large as can be used efficiently in a couple of hours. Put water or additive into the container first, then add the dry ingredients. (If you add the liquid to the mortar, it will be difficult to mix the mortar in the bottom of the container.) Thinset can be handmixed with a small trowel or paddle, but for larger amounts, it's easier to use a heavy-duty drill with a mixer blade. If using a drill, mix thinset at a low speed until it's the consistency of peanut butter. It should apply easily without sagging or running on the wall. If it stiffens excessively while in use, it should be disposed of because adding further liquid at this time will adversely affect its performance.

Apply the thinset to the installation surface with a ⅜-inch notched trowel in a manner akin to frosting a cake (photo 1). Cover an area that can be installed in about 15 minutes. The ridges created by the trowel will flatten out when the ceramic sections are applied, providing good bonding. If the sections are warped or cupped on the back, apply extra thinset to the back sides of them in the same manner. This technique, called "back buttering," ensures that

there are no large voids between the ceramics and the wall (photo 2).

To set vertical sections, place them slightly above their final position in the thinset, force them against the wall, and slide them down into place (photo 3). This action helps to create a more uniform and complete bond. (If working on a vertical surface, remember to set the bottom pieces first and work

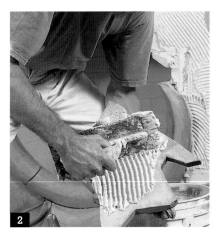

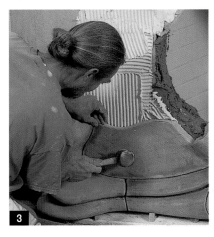

your way up.) Once sections are placed, you can further seat them by tapping them with a rubber mallet.

During this process you may need to use shims or braces in certain areas. To do this, use wedges of wood that fit between the pieces but that project beyond the installation far enough to be later removed *(photo 4)*. When a project spans an opening such as a doorway or fireplace, you may need to install temporary wood braces from the floor to the sections spanning the opening until the adhesive has set *(photo 5)*.

Next, clean any thinset smudges or droppings from the surface, and remove the excess from between the sections. (If you wait until the next day, these areas will be difficult to clean.) Allow the thinset to set overnight.

By the next day the piece should be sufficiently set to allow removal of any shims or braces.

Test pieces to see that they're all firmly in place, then remove any shims and braces.

GROUTING

Grout is a cement product which is available in a wide variety of colors. Like thinset, it comes in both polymer-modified and unmodified forms. Polymer-modified grout is stronger and more water resistant than unmodified grout. If you choose an unmodified version, it can be mixed with a liquid polymer additive. Polymer additive makes grout stronger and therefore more resistant to cracking and staining.

Use a sanded grout for filling in joints between the sections that you've installed. (Unsanded grout tends to shrink, sag, and crack in joints much larger than ⅛ inch wide.) Sand is added to grout for the same reasons that grog is added to clay—to reduce shrinkage. Follow the directions on the bag, and mix the grout with a mixer and blade until it is the consistency of cake batter. The grout will stiffen in the bucket while you are working, so it may be necessary to temper it from time to time by gently remixing it with small additions of water. Unlike thinset, this procedure does not adversely affect grout if it is not repeated excessively.

Grout and thinset are both made with Portland cement, which is extremely caustic. It doesn't take much to burn holes in your skin. For this reason, always wear rubber gloves while grouting. If your hands receive long-term exposure, wash them off with vinegar or lemon juice immediately afterward. The mild acid in these liquids neutralizes the lime in the cement and restores the pH balance in your skin, preventing further damage.

Grout your sections by forcing grout into every seam with a large sponge or glove. If you're working on a horizontal surface, you can pour grout directly from your container onto the surface. Move systematically from one grout line to the next, being certain to fill the joints completely. Remove excess grout and keep grouting. Use your fingertips to force grout into corners and edges, and make sure that there are no voids.

After you've grouted a large area, stop and use a squeezed sponge to start wiping the surface of the piece and clean away excess grout. Don't use an excessive amount of water at this time because it will wash the grout from the seams. As you work, smooth the grout lines. Don't scrub, just wipe and rinse. Use one side of the sponge for one wipe only and then turn it over, because if you

FORCE GROUT INTO EVERY SEAM WITH A LARGE SPONGE OR GLOVE.

USE A SPONGE TO CLEAN AWAY EXCESS GROUT AND CLEAN THE TILE SURFACE.

wipe more than once with the sponge, you'll be wiping grout with grout. After the excess is off, change your water and go back over the piece, removing the finer grout residue. As the grout stiffens, flood the surface with water from a wet sponge without disturbing it. This process helps to harden the grout through a chemical reaction.

Once the surface is thoroughly washed, use wooden pottery tools or sticks to pick away any grout that is trapped in the surface detail. At this point the grout will be almost leather hard and can be carved if necessary. Use a square-tipped stick to carve away a clean edge where a piece terminates against the wall.

Water is usually insufficient to remove the last film of grout from your glazed sections. For this reason, you should return after the grout has dried for a day to wash the film off with vinegar. Rinse off the vinegar residue with water.

You can choose to use a sealer, which will make the grout even more stain and water resistant, after the grouting is finished and dry. Most sealers can be put on after 24 hours. Read the instructions to determine when to apply your brand of sealer

INSTALLING ON ELASTIC MEMBRANE SURFACES

Since the 1980s, there has been a movement toward the use of elastic membrane systems for the construction of everything from houses to shopping centers. In this type of construction, the frame or skeleton of the building is wrapped in a layer of expanded polystyrene that is covered with a thin layer of reinforced rubberized cement.

While the finished surface resembles conventional stucco, this new system is designed to expand and contract with changing temperatures.

Because expanded polystyrene is elastic, and ceramic materials are rigid, the two have very different rates of thermal expansion. If ceramic is set to a membrane surface with thinset, the bond between the two materials will eventually sheer due to differing rates of expansion, and the ceramics will fall off the building. (To picture this, imagine cementing a ceramic tile to a rubber mat and then stretching the mat.)

Therefore, you must create an interface between the building's frame and the ceramics for this type of installation. To do this, use screws long enough to fasten concrete backerboard through the membrane to the frame of the building. (You may need to consult with the building's contractor to find out the thickness of the membrane.)

If the building is commercial, it may be framed with metal studs, in which case you can use self-tapping sheet metal screws (they have a drill head on the tip of each screw). The holes should be well sealed to prevent water intrusion. Once the backerboard is in place, proceed as with the previous installations.

USING MECHANICAL FASTENERS FOR MOVEABLE INSTALLATIONS

Mechanical fasteners can be used for installing architectural projects on walls or masonry so they can be removed later. You may have a client that prefers this method of installation. Knowing about such methods is also important if you're setting up a piece for a gallery or museum exhibition or a commercial show.

You can choose between several different mechanical fasteners and methods:

THE TAB SYSTEM

For a simple and flexible system, you can use a series of tabs that are made of aluminum flashing attached to the backs of the sections. You'll only need to make a few holes in the top sections of the overall piece. The sizes of the tabs are determined by the size of the pieces being hung. Tabs are attached to the uppermost part of each section with a high-grade construction adhesive.

To undertake this method, cut pieces of flashing between 3 and 6 inches square, depending on the size and weight of your

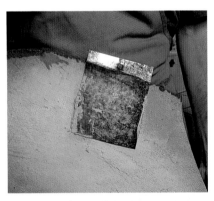

pieces. Using an ample amount of adhesive, attach roughly two-thirds of the flashing to the back of the piece, leaving the rest for attaching the piece to the wall. To accelerate adhesion, apply adhesive to the flashing, press it into place on the back of the piece, and remove it. Then when the adhesive is nearly dry to the touch, put it in place and press firmly.

Begin installing the lower sections when you're finished fitting the sections with tabs. Use an electric screwdriver and screws that are appropriate for the particular wall that you're hanging. (If you're installing on drywall, you'll need to use drywall inserts.) Cover the tabs as you overlap subsequent pieces.

As an alternative to drywall inserts, you can also mount to a piece of plywood placed between the project and the wall. Cut a piece slightly smaller than the dimensions of the piece you're installing, and mount it on the wall's studs. Mount sections directly into the plywood with drywall screws.

ATTACHING SECTIONS WITH SCREWS

You can also fasten sections impermanently by creating holes in each section in order

to screw sections to the wall. These may be concealed in the design or used as part of it. Countersink the holes so that the head of the screw does not protrude or chip the glaze.

To do this, create a hole in the wet clay with the screw that you plan to use, then create a circular indentation in the clay surrounding the hole by pressing the clay with the end of a larger nail or dowel.

When the piece is dry and glazed, turn the sections over and clean out the holes that you've punched, because they may have accumulated clay around the edges.

SELF-TAPPING CONCRETE SCREWS

If you're attaching a piece to a masonry surface, use self-tapping concrete screws. To do this, first create a plywood interface as described in the tab section. Screw the plywood to the wall with self-tapping concrete screws, before attaching sections to the plywood. To mount an interface with these screws, drill pilot holes deeper than the screws with the drill bit that accompanies them. (If no bit comes with yours, you'll need to get a bit of the size that's indicated on the box.)

Top & above: TABS MADE OF ALUMINUM FLASHING CAN BE USED FOR INSTALLING MOVEABLE INSTALLATIONS SUCH AS GALLERY EXHIBITIONS.

CREATING HOLES IN THE WET CLAY MAKES IT SIMPLE TO SCREW THE PIECES INTO PLACE LATER.

FOR INSTALLATION ON MASONRY, ATTACH A PLYWOOD INTERFACE WITH SELF-TAPPING CONCRETE SCREWS.

Chapter Five

THE
PROJECTS

The following chapter will introduce you to the basics of making sinks and pedestals as well as detailed steps that show the building and installation of a countertop, a door surround, and a fireplace at Stonehaus. Keep in mind that these projects are based upon all of the techniques that were covered in chapter two. The techniques are interchangeable. In other words, you might use a box-built column on a door surround, although you'll see it incorporated into a fireplace surround in this chapter. As you learn the vocabulary of architectural ceramics, you'll be amazed at the ways in which you can alter and use techniques imaginatively. So, be bold! Don't limit yourself to what we teach you, but use it as a springboard.

MAKING SINKS & PEDESTALS

Before you undertake making a sink, you should familiarize yourself with its parts. Most of us have a tendency to think of sinks as simply being bowls with a hole in the bottom, but there is much more to a sink because of its relationship to plumbing fixtures.

First you should know that the size of the drain hole in the bottom of the sink is reflective of the drainpipe's diameter that has been standardized by the plumbing industry. The distance from the bottom of the sink to the outside of the overflow bowl (a smaller bowl attached under the sink that is necessary in order to meet plumbing codes) is determined by the length of the drainpipe. These factors will affect the size of the drain hole that you create and the depth of your overflow bowl. You must be aware of them in order to create a sink that will function correctly.

You should also know the dimensions of the plumbing fixtures that you're going to be using before beginning the sink. They come together as a kit that includes the drainpipe. Make note of the faucet's length and height, and be certain that it is of a size that works for the sink once it's installed.

Beginning lower left, page 48, and continuing clockwise on page 49:

PETER KING (Pensacola, Florida), *High Tide*, 5 ft., 6½ in. (1.5 m),1996; glazed stoneware, handbuilt and tile pressed; Δ5-6.

LEE DAVIS (Brasstown, North Carolina), *untitled*, 1997; sink, 14 x 14 x 6 in. (35 x 35 x 15 cm); tile surface, 2 x 6 ft. (60 x 180 cm); stoneware; wheel-thrown sink, handbuilt tiles; Δ8. Photo by artist

KATHY TRIPLETT (Weaverville, North Carolina), *untitled*, 1998; 8 x 3 x 1 ft. (20 x 7.5 x 2.5 cm); brown and white mid-range clay; slab-built, extruded; Δ4. Photo by Tim Barnwell

MARY KAY DAVIS (Baton Rouge, Louisiana), *untitled*, bathroom,1998; 10 x 11 x 14 ft. (3 x 3.3 x 4.2 m); white earthenware; terra sigillata; slip-cast columns; wheel-thrown sink and light fixture, column capital and base; slab shelf and field tiles; slab and extruded floor, ceiling, and chair rail border; bas-relief door decoration; Δ04-Δ06. Photo by artist

In the following section, the steps for making a sink using a cast mold are explained. Throwing a sink on the wheel is an alternative to the drape mold, but is much more difficult. You can make a draped sink that has a rim that is thrown onto the body after it is draped, or one that has a rim that is a part of the original draped slab. Both rims support the sink once it is dropped into the countertop.

The last section will describe how to make pedestal sinks. Pedestals are made and fired separately from the sink bowl. You can throw a pedestal on the wheel or hand build a pedestal, depending on your experience and preference.

POURING A SINK MOLD

To make a ceramic sink using a mold, you must first find a form to use for casting a mold of the shape and size that you want. This mold, often called a *drape* or *hump mold*, will be used later for draping a slab of clay that will form the sink. Check a kitchen or home-supply store for something suitable to use, such as large mixing bowls, a round-bottomed wok, a food container, "lazy Susan" cover, or light fixture covers made of metal or plastic. The mold form for a bathroom sink should be 13 to 15 inches in diameter to make a standard-sized sink, and the bottom must be rounded, not flat. With the addition of a rim, the sink will end up being larger when installed in the countertop. For instance, if you add a 1½-inch rim, the sink's diameter will end up being 3 inches larger overall, or 16 to 18 inches wide.

In choosing the size of the sink to make, you must consider the final layout of the countertop that you'll be installing. In order for the sink to fit into the countertop, leave enough room between the sink and the backsplash for the faucets. It's best to place the sink as close to the front edge of the counter as possible in order to make it comfortable to use. Because of the many styles of faucets available, you'll need to calculate the space behind the sink according to the specifics of your situation. The size and placement of the faucets may determine the size of the sink that you'll make, and therefore the size of the mold.

Once you've selected the master mold that you'd like to cast into a drape mold, prepare the container for plaster casting by coating it with vegetable shortening or oil. (Avoid animal-based products because they don't have the same mold release properties.) If the mold is rounded, you can level it by setting it on the rim of a five-gallon bucket, or a bed of sand, and adjusting its position.

Now you're ready to mix the plaster for pouring into the mold. Allow the plaster to slake for a few minutes, or stand, so that it can begin to dissolve, before mixing *(photo 1)*. If mixing plaster by hand, stir it until the lumps disappear. You can also blend the plaster with a mixer blade on a drill for around two and a half minutes at low rpm's *(photo 2)*. After mixing, pour the plaster into the mold immediately *(photo 3)*.

SINK DRAPE MOLDS ARE MADE BY CASTING PLASTER IN AN OBJECT SUCH AS A LARGE BOWL OR WOK.

When making a sink mold, you can reduce the amount of plaster needed to fill the mold, and make the final mold lighter and easier to handle, by pressing a child's plastic ball or a plastic container that has been oiled into the plaster to create a partially hollow mold (photo 4). If you decide to do this, remember that you'll be displacing some plaster when you submerge the object, so experiment with a lower level of plaster until you get the right amount to fill the mold to just below the rim once the object is in place.

To hold the ball or bowl in place, position a small board on it to press it down into the plaster and, if needed, anchor the board with bricks on either end while the plaster sets. Press the ball halfway into the plaster, but no further, so that it will be easy to remove later. In about 20 minutes, after the plaster has set, invert the mold and its container, allowing the mold to drop out. If the mold doesn't fall out immediately, tip the mold on a board, tap it gently on top, and let it drop while keeping your hands under the mold's edge to prevent damaging it. After removing it, lightly scrub the mold with a soft brush and water so that it won't leave a plaster residue on the clay that can later prevent glaze from bonding to the surface. Before

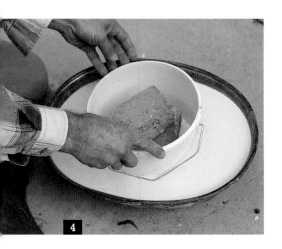

using it, allow the mold to cure at about 12° C (120° F) to accelerate the curing so that the plaster can harden completely. Don't overheat the mold because it will begin to disintegrate.

DRAPING THE MOLD

After making a mold that conforms to the inside dimensions of the sink that you want to make, center it on a potter's wheel or banding wheel. Roll a slab that is ¾-inch thick and large enough to drape over the mold. To find the sink's curved diameter, use a tape measure to measure from one side of the mold across the top to the other. Then use a needle tool to cut out a circular piece of clay of this diameter from the slab. Lift this piece of clay, then drape and center it on the mold (photo 5). Work the clay from the top down by pressing and forming it to the mold with your hands (photo 6). If the clay gathers, join it together by pounding it and then removing any excess clay.

Turn the wheel and further conform the clay to the mold by making several passes over the surface with your fingers or a flexible smoothing tool. To make a slab-rimmed sink, trim the circumference of the draped slab while spinning the wheel to leave a rim of clay on the bat of the width you want (photo 7).

If you plan to install faucets in the rim rather than behind it, you'll do best to choose a slab-rimmed design because the resulting rim is wide and flat-surfaced. To decide the width of rim that you need, you must first choose the faucets that you plan to use in order to know the diameter of the pipes. Building a 2- to 2½-inch rim will allow you to place almost any faucet comfortably, since most faucet pipes have a diameter of about 1½ inches.

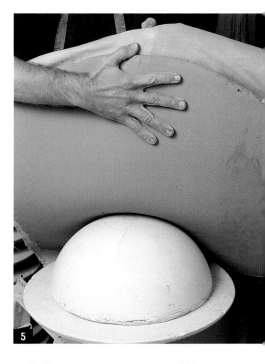

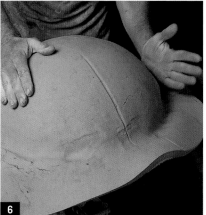

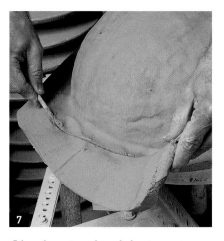

After forming the slab rim, reinforce the inside corner of the rim with a coil or strip of slab (photo 8). Clean and compress the corner with a scraping tool (photo 9) before trimming the edge of the rim with a needle tool.

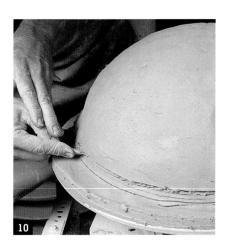

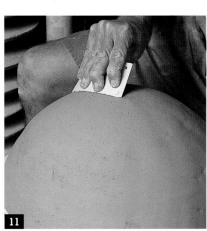

To add holes in the slab rim for the hot and cold water faucets, use the template that comes with them for the purpose of establishing the size of the holes. Decide where you want to place the faucets in relationship to the overflow hole. Add clay shrinkage to the size of the template, and cut the holes to this size in the rim.

To make a sink with a wheel-thrown, applied rim, trim away the excess clay where it meets the bat *(photo 10)*, and smooth the clay with a flexible plastic rib *(photo 11)*.

MAKING THE OVERFLOW BOWL

To make the sink's overflow bowl, wheel-throw a ¾-inch-thick bowl about 5 to 6 inches in diameter, with the depth equal to the length of the drainpipe that you'll be using. (Most drainpipes are about 2½ inches long.) To achieve the same result as a thrown bowl, you can make a small drape mold of the size that you need, and drape a bowl. Make either bowl with a rim that turns outward about ¾ inch. This lip will be used to attach the overflow bowl to the sink later.

Next, using the overflow bowl's diameter, mark a circle in the clay all the way around the sink to indicate where the overflow bowl will join the sink *(photo 12)*. Score the inside rim of the bowl and the area on the sink where the rim will join the bowl *(photo 13)*. Invert the overflow bowl on the sink, and then turn the wheel while you press the two together *(photos 14, 15)*.

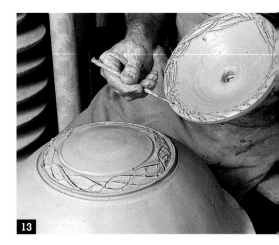

Cutting the Drain and Overflow Holes

To make a drain hole, determine the exact center of the overflow bowl. Draw a circle around this point that is about 1⅞ inches in diameter. (This size is large enough to accommodate the drainpipe after the clay shrinks.) Cut the hole out with a needle tool (photo 16), and trim away the excess clay around the top of the bowl (photo 17). Reshape the bowl by smoothing the top of it while turning the wheel (photo 18). To make a clean hole all the way through the sink, slowly turn and immerse a piece of 1⅞-inch pipe into the drain hole and through the overflow bowl to the sink underneath (photo 19). If you don't use a pipe, cut all the way through the overflow bowl and sink with a knife or needle tool. Smooth the edge of this hole to finish it.

To cut the overflow opening, use a needle tool to start at the lower edge of any point on the overflow bowl, and cut out an arched opening about 1½ inches high at the arch's apex and 1½ inches wide (photo 20).

Making the Overflow Channel

Next you'll be forming a flap out of clay that will serve as an overflow channel that will run from the overflow bowl and up the outside of the sink to the drain hole. To do this, score around the rim of the arched opening in the overflow bowl in preparation for joining the overflow channel. From the base of the overflow opening, extend parallel tracks down the face of the sink. Score and slip these paths for joining the overflow channel (photo 21).

To make the overflow channel, roll a ⅝-inch slab and cut out a rectangle that is around 5 by 11 inches (this may vary depending on the depth of the sink). This width of slab is easy to form into a tube and fasten to the sink, but thick enough to glaze in the greenware state without splitting. Trim one end of the clay rectangle into an arched shape that covers the arched opening in the overflow bowl (photo 22). Score the

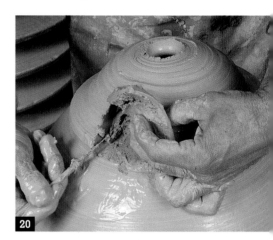

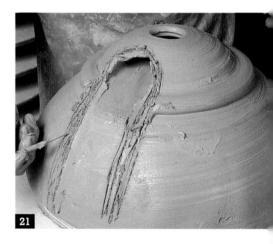

edges of the arched piece of clay, and then apply slip. Take the slab in both hands with the score marks face down, and form an inverted U-shape by pushing the sides of the slab toward each other to create a bulge, or tunnel, in the middle. Bend the scored edges out about ¾ inch, so that they can be attached to the overflow bowl and sink.

Attach the arched end first over the hole in the overflow bowl, lining up the scored areas (photo 23). Attach the overflow channel to the outside of the sink bowl by pressing the scored part of the slab against the scored paths on the sink bowl (photo 24). Shape the tube and join the seams with your fingers or a sponge where the channel meets the sink (photo 25).

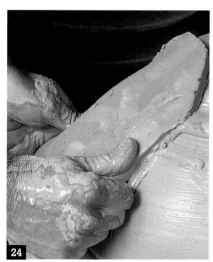

DRYING THE SINK ON THE MOLD

Leave the sink with the overflow bowl and channel on the mold to stiffen overnight. When the clay has stiffened to the touch, just before it becomes leather hard, it can be worked without deforming it excessively. You can prepare to remove it from the mold at this point.

The fact that little shrinkage occurs during the wet to leather-hard stage of drying is very helpful when working with drape-molded forms, because it is possible to leave the draped form on the mold until it is almost leather hard without cracking it.

MAKING A CHUCK TO RECEIVE THE SINK

Prepare for inverting and removing the sink from the mold by forming a doughnut, or, chuck, out of soft clay, with a

hole in the center just large enough to hold the overflow bowl. Center it on the wheel, and indent the clay to form a channel that will accommodate the overflow tube when the sink is set into it (photos 26-28).

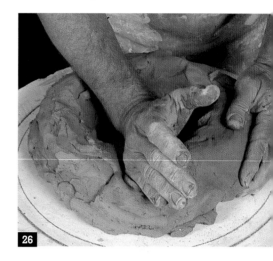

REMOVING THE SINK FROM THE MOLD

When the sink is stiff enough, break it loose from the mold by lifting it from the bottom edge, using your fingers to pry around the edges in order to loosen it. If the clay flexes noticeably when it is lifted from the mold, gently press it back into shape on the mold and allow it to stiffen more. When you have lifted the sink from the mold, invert it and place it in the chuck.

LEVELING AND CENTERING THE SINK ON THE WHEEL

The top of the sink must now be leveled and centered. To level it, spin the wheel and check the edge of the sink to see if it is level. If it isn't, keep gently adjusting the sink in the chuck by rolling the high side down and low side up. Keep adjusting the sink until you see that it isn't wavering when you spin the wheel.

Center the sink by gently moving the doughnut chuck and sink as a unit. Spin the wheel and check for the center with your hands locked together and firmly positioned above it, while guiding one finger slowly toward the edge of the spinning bowl. Adjust the side your finger touches first away from center. Repeat the process until the sink is centered on the wheel.

Fasten the clay chuck firmly to the wheel by squeezing the bottom edge down onto the wheel with a thumb or the heel of your hand. Repeat this process more gently to fasten the chuck to the sink. (It's important not to fuse the chuck to the bottom of the sink, so that you can remove it later.)

If you've made a sink with a draped rim, allow the sink to dry

on the chuck until it's ready to be glazed and fired. (For further instructions on a draped-rim sink, skip the next sections concerning applying a thrown rim, and move to "Making the Overflow Hole and Finishing the Sink" on page 59.)

If you've made a sink without a rim, leave the sink on the wheel in the chuck in preparation for applying a hand-thrown rim which will be explained in the following section.

PREPARING THE SINK FOR THE RIM

To prepare the sink for attaching the rim, trim the top of the sink with a loop tool while spinning the wheel (photo 29). Continue to use the loop tool to carve away about half the thickness of the sink's inside edge to form a ledge about ½ inch wide and ⅜ inch deep. (You'll attach the sink's rim to

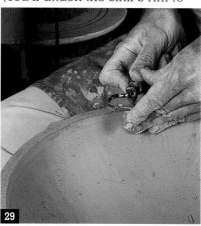

this ledge later.) Score and slip the ledge in preparation for adding the rim (photo 30).

THROWING A RIM ON A SINK

To throw an applied section, such as a sink rim, requires well-tempered plastic clay and good throwing skills. You must create the equivalent of a cylinder of de-aired pugged clay

through the process of wedging and kneading it.

Start by measuring the circumference of the edge of your sink with a tape measure. (To make the following explanation simpler, we'll use a circumference of 3 feet that correlates with a common-sized sink. Don't forget to substitute the actual circumference of your sink rim.)

Thoroughly wedge and knead 15 to 20 pounds of clay. Slam the clay on the wedging table at a 45° angle, with the trailing edge hitting the table first. Rotate the clay a quarter turn and slam it out again *(photos 31-33)*. Repeat this process until the clay elongates to about 3 feet. Begin twisting the clay clockwise while rolling it on the table *(photo 34)*. Continue twisting and rolling the clay until you have obtained a cylinder about 3 inches in diameter and slightly longer than 3 feet *(photo 35)*.

Place gauge boards on either side of the clay cylinder about 6 inches apart that are 1¼ inches thick and longer than the circumference of the rim. These will be used to roll the clay to its proper thickness. Use a rolling pin to flatten the coil into the space between the boards *(photos 36, 37)*.

Once the clay is flattened to the thickness of the boards, use one of the boards as a straightedge. With a needle tool, cut a straight line the length of the coil, close to one edge. Measure 3 inches across from this edge before marking and trimming the clay again *(photo 38)*. The resulting slab is a strip of clay that is 1¼ inch thick, 3 inches wide, and slightly over 3 feet long. Make a strip that is longer than you need, to give you enough clay to lap over where the head and tail of the rim are joined together.

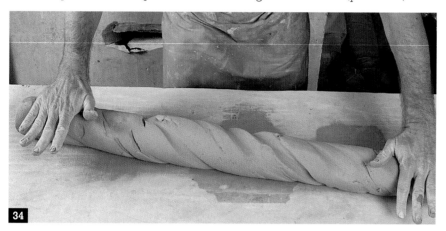

34

35

37

36

38

THROWING THE RIM ONTO THE SINK BOWL

Beginning with a tight turn of the clay at one end, roll the rim up into a compact spiral (photo 39) to make the clay easier to handle during the next step.

While holding the clay spiral inside the bowl with one hand, unroll a portion of it and, while slowly moving the wheel, begin pressing it vertically into the ledge that you carved earlier on the inside edge of the sink (photos 40, 41). Where the rim overlaps, make 45° angled cuts that fit together so that this seam has the same thickness as the rest of the rim (photo 42). If the rim is either thicker or thinner at this seam, correct this by scraping or filling areas to obtain the same thickness before beginning to throw.

To begin throwing the rim once it's firmly attached, make a firm vertical pull with your hands on either side of the rim (photo 43). After the first pull, spin the wheel and use a needle tool to trim about ½ to ¾ inch of clay off of the top of the rim to eliminate irregularities (photo 44). To continue, spin the sink while forcing the rim outward into place around the edge of the sink bowl. Press the rim outward from the inside of the bowl with one hand while counterbalancing the pressure from the underside of the rim with the other hand (photo 45). Make a few more pulls to establish the profile and dimensions of the rim. Flatten the outer edge of the rim with a tool or fingers (photo 46). (Don't overdo throwing at this phase. As with any wheel-thrown form, it's easy to overwork the rim, and any irregularities will tend to become more pronounced with too much throwing.)

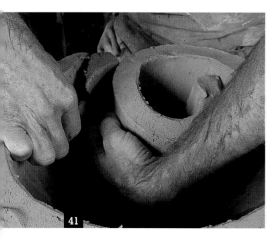

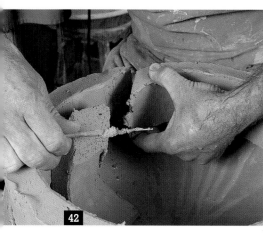

After the rim is in place, the area that joins together the sink bowl and the applied rim can either be smoothed or accentuated. To finish throwing the rim, squeeze the upper edge of the rim out to establish a flat ledge that is 1 to 1½ inches wide. This will allow the sink to rest on its rim when installed in the countertop and also provide some leeway in the size of the countertop hole. (To make a splash guard for the sink, you can throw a rounded bead from the bottom inside edge of the applied rim.)

MAKING THE OVERFLOW HOLE AND FINISHING THE SINK

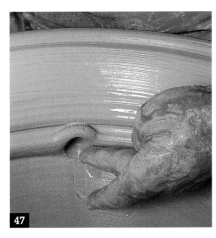

To make the overflow hole, mark the outline of a ⅞-inch diameter hole inside the sink where the rim and bowl interface (photo 47). (In most cases, a ⅞-inch diameter hole is adequate to prevent overflow even if the faucet is left on at full volume.) Check the hole's position on the outside of the sink to make sure that this hole will access the overflow channel once it's cut. After checking the hole's placement, carve the hole out with a needle tool or use a pipe of that size to cut it out (photo 48). Smooth the hole so that the edges that face inside the bowl are slightly rounded.

To finish the sink, smooth the interior with a rubber rib. A finishing touch on the drain hole will allow the rim of the drain to seat in the bottom of the sink so that it doesn't hold water. To do this, create a small circular indentation about ¼-inch wide and ⅛-inch deep in which to rest the drain's flange by turning the sink while resting two forefingers in the drain hole and using your thumb to depress a small circular valley.

REMOVING THE SINK FROM THE CHUCK

Leave the sink in its chuck until the rim is leather hard, then remove it from the chuck and invert it on its rim. If you discover that the underside edge of the rim isn't perfectly flat, trim it with a loop tool so that it is. Allow it to dry to the bone-dry stage while resting on its rim to prevent it from warping.

GLAZING THE SINK

After the sink is bone dry, it's ready for glazing. Lightly sand any sharp edges, then blow the resulting dust off with compressed air, or wipe the surface with a damp sponge.

Glaze can be applied to the sink by spraying or pouring. To pour, plug the drain hole from the outside of the sink with a cork. Tilt the bowl at a 45° angle. Pour approximately ½ to 1 gallon of glaze into the bowl. Roll the bowl while supporting it with both hands to distribute the glaze. To glaze the rim, pour glaze out of the sink and over the sides into a glaze bucket, while continuing to roll the bowl. Allow the glaze to run out the overflow hole and into the overflow channel and bowl to cover those areas. To complete the job, leave some glaze in the bowl, swirl it around, position the sink over the glaze bucket, and remove the cork to allow the glaze to run out the drain hole. This process insures that the entire surface is thoroughly coated with glaze, including the inside of the overflow channel and bowl, which prevents possible leaks after the sink is installed.

After the glaze dries, clean any excess glaze away from the bottom of the drain hole, and seat the sink on a bed of grog for firing. If glaze flows into the drain hole during firing, it can usually be chipped or ground off. You can also fire the sink on a closed-bottomed chuck. This will allow excess glaze to run out of the sink and into the chuck.

PEDESTAL SINKS

Pedestal sinks are made in two parts, so that the drain and faucet can be installed in the sink before it is set into place on the pedestal. This construction facilitates removal and repair should there be any plumbing problems. The pedestal houses the drainpipe and its P-trap.

A THROWN PEDESTAL FOR SUPPORTING A SINK CREATES AN AESTHETICALLY PLEASING CURVED LINE.

Faucets for pedestal sinks may be set into the sink's rim, wall-mounted using a bracket, or mounted in the wall. Consult a licensed plumber before building the sink, and get assistance for any changes that may need to be made to the plumbing.

To make a pedestal sink, use the drape mold system (see pages 51-59) for the sink portion, using a ¾ inch slab. Make the overflow bowl with a larger-diameter rim (use about a 7- to 8-inch diameter with a 1¼-inch-wide rim), so that it can sit in the pedestal.

When applying the overflow bowl to the sink, make a deep depression at least ¾ inch wide where the rim of the overflow bowl attaches to the drape mold sink. Leave a thick bead of clay at the outer edge of the rim. Just as with a lidded jar, this groove and bead form the seat for the pedestal. Measure the outside diameter of the groove with a set of calipers to determine the exact outside diameter that needs to be used to form the top of the pedestal. The pedestal itself can be thrown or slab-built.

You can change the height of the sink by adjusting the height of the pedestal. To determine the height of your pedestal, you must first decide the finished height for your sink and add clay shrinkage. (A standard sink is 31 to 32 inches from the floor to the rim, but you can make it any height that is comfortable for you or your client.) From this measurement, subtract the distance from the bottom of the drape-molded sink (without the depth of the overflow bowl since it drops into the pedestal) to the top of the sink rim. The resulting measurement is the height of the pedestal in wet clay. Whether throwing or slab-building the pedestal, the walls should be at least ¾-inch thick to be strong and durable. The pedestal should have a wide base that is between 14 and 18 inches in diameter to make it stable and proportional.

Making a Wheel-Thrown Pedestal

You must have experience in throwing vessels on the wheel before attempting a wheel-thrown pedestal. If this method isn't the right choice for you, read the next section on slab-building a pedestal.

At Stonehaus, we create the pedestal in two parts to make it easier to throw and handle. The stem of this pedestal resembles that of a wine goblet—it tapers quickly from the base and becomes vertical before flaring slightly at the top so that it can accommodate the sink. The wide base gives it stability while the slender proportions make it aesthetically pleasing.

Throwing the Bottom Section

The bottom section of the pedestal is thrown to at least half the height of the finished pedestal. This first section has some leeway in height, because you can always make the top taller or shorter. This section should end up being approximately 14 to 18 inches wide at the base.

To begin making the bottom of the pedestal, center and open about 25 to 30 pounds of clay on the wheel. Leave a ¾-inch-thick bottom at the base, and spread the clay until you've obtained the desired base diameter. Incline the walls inward as you pull them up, reducing their diameter rapidly. Taper off until the sides become parallel and are 5 to 6 inches apart. Make the last several inches of the walls equidistant from each other; doing this will make it much easier to form an imperceptible union with the top section of the pedestal later.

Throwing the Top Section

The top section of the pedestal is a hollow, open-ended form with no base. When throwing this form, remember that the bottom of it will become the top of the pedestal and the seat for the sink; therefore, its diameter must match that of the indentation you've created in the sink's overflow bowl. The pedestal tapers out only slightly toward the top to accommodate the sink's diameter and lend stability to the pedestal. The pedestal should end up being about 5 to 6 inches wide at the point where it connects to the other section, and 7 to 8 inches at the top where it meets the sink.

Throw the form upside down on a bat that can later be removed from the wheel head and inverted for placing the top section on the bottom section. Open the clay up all the way to the surface of the bat, leaving a little clay around the inner rim of the base of the wall. This foot prevents the clay from detaching from the wheel while throwing the walls and adheres the form to the bat so that it can be inverted later.

Raise the walls of this section to a slightly greater height than needed for the pedestal. Check the diameter of the bottom section's top rim with a pair of calipers, then adjust the diameter of the top of the cylinder that you've thrown to make sure that it's the same. Cut off any excess clay, leaving a clean squared-off top exactly the same diameter as the top of the base section. Leave this section fastened to the bat.

JOINING THE SECTIONS

Allow both sections to stiffen to the point that they aren't quite leather hard and don't distort. Thoroughly score, but don't slip, the top edges where the two pieces are to be joined. Lift the top section by the bat with both hands and invert it, so that the section hangs from the bat. Position the piece carefully over the base section and align it with the bottom section. Using a needle tool, "sew" the pieces together without using

slip. Fill and scrape the seam between the two sections.

Place a level across the bat to make certain that the rim is the same height all the way around. If it is slightly off, fine-tune it by pushing down slightly on the higher side of the bat. To remove the bat from the top of the pedestal, brace yourself against the bat and pull a cutting wire across the top edge of the section flush with the bat. Remove the bat. To add strength to the union of the two pieces, reinforce the inside joint of the cylinder by reaching inside and building up a bead of clay at the seam.

FINISHING THE PEDESTAL

Trim any excess clay away from the pedestal's top, and cut away a negative profile of the overflow channel so that it fits into the groove in the sink's overflow bowl. After cutting this notch, extend this cut area into a 2-inch-wide parallel slot down the backside of the pedestal to accommodate the drainpipe and P-trap. (Check the layout of the particular plumbing that you'll be using to determine where the lower end of your cut in the back of the pedestal must be.) Leave a tab of clay bridging the slot near the top of the pedestal to prevent this section from warping in the firing. The overflow channel of the sink will key into the top of this slot. Cut holes in the bottom of the pedestal so it can be screwed or bolted to the floor upon installation.

Glaze and fire the sink and pedestal separately. Afterwards, remove the tab, bridging the slot with an angle grinder equipped with a dry-cutting diamond blade.

The installation of your pedestal sink should be coordinated with a licensed plumber. After the pedestal is set in place, you can stabilize it more by running a bead of clear silicone caulk between it and the sink before placing them together.

MAKING HANDBUILT PEDESTALS

A wheel-thrown pedestal is pleasing to the eye, but it isn't the only way to construct a ceramic pedestal. There are as many ways to make a pedestal as there are to make a pot. Any vertical clay construction has the potential to serve as a

A DRAPED COLUMN FORM MAKES AN UNOB-TRUSIVE, FUNCTIONAL PEDESTAL FOR A SINK.

pedestal for a sink. They can be thrown, slab-built, coiled, or pressed into a mold. In our work at Stonehaus, we've come up with several quick-to-build pedestals onto which you can apply any number of surface treatments. If you use one of these ideas, don't limit yourself to the suggestions you see here. After learning the basics, you'll probably want to develop your own variation and incorporate other techniques.

You can build a simple column-shaped pedestal for your sink by rolling a slab of clay around a pipe. This pedestal provides support for the sink but doesn't hide any plumbing except the drain pipe, which runs through the center of it. PVC pipe works well for building this pedestal because it is lighter than most available forms of pipe and is easy to find in various diameters. An option that works well for making a tall cylinder is residential sewer pipe, which is 4 inches in diameter and comes in 20-foot lengths. It's relatively expensive, but you may be able to get free scraps of it from a construction site or plumbing supply house.

To keep the clay from sticking to the pipe, you can wrap any pipe that you use with paper (newspaper works well) before wrapping it with clay. Overlap the paper and tape it to itself, not the pipe, when preparing it for the slab. If the pipe is 6 inches or larger in diameter, you can also use shortening to grease the pipe so that the clay form is easy to remove later.

To begin making a handbuilt pedestal, roll out a slab on a moveable piece of canvas and leave it attached. (I normally use a ¾-inch slab because this thickness is both easy to form around a tube and substantial

enough to make a functional pedestal.) The wetness of the clay that you use is important. If it is too soft, it will slump when the pipe is in an upright position. If it is too dry, it will crack when you wrap it around the cylinder.

Measure the circumference of your pipe with a tape measure, and decide upon the height of your pedestal. Then add the clay's shrinkage. Cut the slab into a rectangle wider than the circumference of the pipe and long enough for the height of the pedestal, leaving a couple of inches of exposed canvas at one end of the slab. The extra width of the slab will allow you to roll it onto itself once you have wrapped it around the pipe. Score the edge of the slab that will overlap to form the seam.

Place the pipe on the slab, grab the canvas, and use it to roll the slab tightly around the pipe to form a clay cylinder. After the slab is lapped onto itself, peel the canvas away. Roll the pipe onto the overlapping clay seam and rock it back and forth, applying pressure to fuse the clay together. The vertical seam can be eliminated or accentuated. Cut away any excess slab, and stand the tube and clay cylinder upright on a slab large enough to form a bottom for the clay cylinder. Cut away any excess clay from this bottom slab, "sew" the two together, and remove the pipe from the clay cylinder. The entire surface can receive any number of treatments.

For a variation on this rolled cylinder technique, drape a slab over a half-cylindrical form as described in the section entitled "Building Tubular Forms" on pages 28-30. After creating a half-column arched shape of the

height that you want, cut a long rectangular slab that fits the outer dimensions of the back of the pedestal. Score and "sew" this section to the back of the half column. Allow the construction to stiffen to the point that it is firm but still malleable. Stand it up on a slab slightly larger than the base of the pedestal, and cut out a piece of clay to form the bottom of it. "Sew" the base to the pedestal. Cut a slot in the back for the sink's P-trap before finishing the surface of the clay.

BUILDING COUNTERTOPS

Countertops can be tricky to make and install, especially if you are building the counter and backsplash as a single unit in the wet clay (see the project that follows for an example of this procedure). Begin by taking careful site measurements including the width and length of the counter, the height of the backsplash (include windows, cabinets, or other features that affect the layout), and the size of the sink.

When installing a new sink in your countertop, use the cardboard template that accompanies it for cutting a sink hole of the correct size in the wet clay (don't forget to add the clay's shrinkage). If covering an existing counter, measure and record the size of the sink hole that already exists to determine the size of the hole that you cut. If replacing an old sink with a new, smaller sink, it may be necessary to replace the old top to accomodate the new sink .

The standard substrate for a countertop is ¾-inch plywood, which is usually of a higher grade than construction plywood. Although it is often used for countertops, composition or particle board are not recommended as substrates since they will decompose over time when exposed to water.

Top: **PETER KING** (Pensacola, Florida), *Waves*, 12 x 10 ft. (3.6 x 3 m), 1995; glazed stoneware, slab built; Δ5-6.

Above: **PETER KING** (Pensacola, Florida), *Desert Rain*, 10 ft. 9 in. x 3 ft. 3 in. (3.2 m x 97 cm), 1998; glazed stoneware, handbuilt and slab built; Δ5-6.

COUNTERTOP PROJECT

This L-shaped countertop and backsplash with a rounded, bold front edge was designed and made by my wife, Xinia Marin, who is a ceramics professor at the University of Costa Rica. The top has been cut in a diamond pattern to represent cultivated fields, and the backsplash has a low relief depicting the view from her front yard in Costa Rica.

The backsplash measures 17½ inches by 74 inches under the cabinet and 6½ inches by 80 inches under the window. The countertop sink area is 27½ inches wide by 57 inches long. The sink measures 31½ inches by 21 inches. The other section of countertop set at a right angle to the sink area measures 27½ inches wide by 74 inches long.

Making this countertop involves laying a base slab, drawing in the clay, layering and cutting to create relief, and embossing. All of these techniques have been discussed in chapter two in more depth.

LAYING THE BASE SLAB

1. Use an overhead projector to project the original drawing for the countertop's design onto a piece of 4-6 mm clear plastic hung on the wall. Adjust the projector until the image is blown up

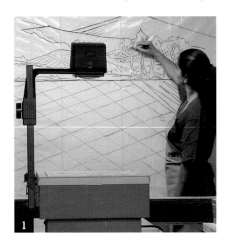

to the size needed to cover the backsplash and counter areas. Don't forget to add clay shrinkage. Trace the lines with a permanent marker. (Notice the dividing line that is drawn between what will become the vertical backsplash section and the horizontal countertop section.)

2. Configure tables and add vertical side pieces to accommodate the countertop and backsplash as it is built in the wet clay. Clean the surface with a damp sponge in preparation for laying the base slab.

3. Spread a thin bed of grog over the surface.

4, 5. Roll ⅝-inch-thick slabs to form sections of the countertop's base slab. Position the slabs

gently while supporting them from underneath. Flip them onto the grogged surface, allowing enough of the clay to hang over the edge and form the lip of the countertop. Overlap the edges of the slabs as you add them.

6. Fold the slabs over the edge of the table and press them into place to form the countertop's lip.

7. Smooth the countertop lip with a serrated scaper. The

8

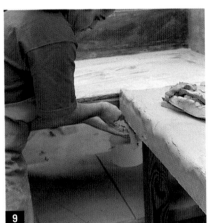

9

10

11

pressure of the scraper helps to adhere the slab to the edge of the table.

8. Reinforce the edge between the counter and its lip by adding an additional coil of clay and roughly smoothing it with your fingers.

9. Trim away the excess clay from the underside of the table edge.

10. Follow the same procedure to lay out additional slabs to form the remainder of the countertop's base slab. Overlap the seams for joining later.

11. Pound the slabs together at the seams.

12. Rake the seams using your fingers to level the over-

12

lapped clay and assist in joining the seams.

13, 14. Use trowels and drywall scrapers to scrape the seams and establish a smooth, uniform surface.

15-19. Fill in blank areas of the countertop surface with strips of clay before scraping and smoothing them to the same level as the rest of the surface.

20. Press clay firmly into the corners to insure a substantial bond with the backsplash slab to be added next.

13

14

21,22. Flip slabs supported by canvas onto the vertical backboard that will be used to form the backsplash of the countertop.

23. Fold the slab several inches over the top edge of the backboard to hold it in place.

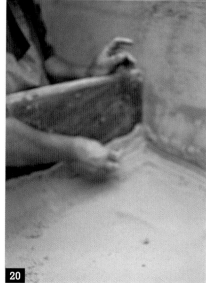

24-26. After the slab has been affixed to the backboard, peel away the canvas and fasten the backsplash slab to the countertop slab by pressing the two firmly together where they join at the corner. Join the seams by smoothing them with your fingertips.

27. Further adhere the base slab by pressing it firmly with an ink roller.

28. Continue joining slabs to complete the backsplash's base slab.

29. Use a measuring tape or ruler to mark off the width of the countertop's edge.

30,31. Remove the excess clay at the bottom of the edge with a straightedge and needle tool.

32. Cut a strip of slab the width of the countertop edge. Score and slip the edge, then press the strip into place. Adding this clay provides the extra thickness needed for the draw tool to be used later, as well as making a countertop edge with a bolder, more substantial look.

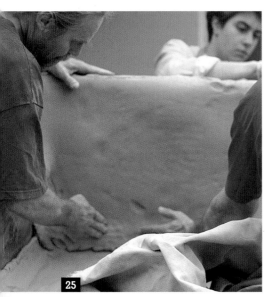

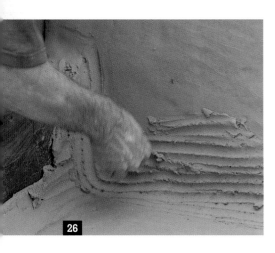

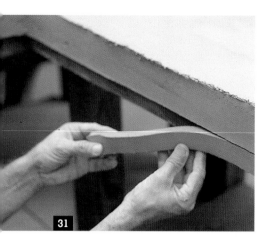

31

32

33

34

35

36

33. Smooth the top edge between the countertop and the joined slab with your fingertips.

34. Scrape and smooth the counter's edge in preparation for shaping it with a draw tool.

35. Shape the front edge with a draw tool cut to produce a rounded countertop lip that is aesthetically pleasing and comfortable to lean into while working on the counter and at the sink.

36. Between passes, squeeze water on the surface with a sponge to lubricate it in preparation for the next pass of the draw tool.

CREATING THE RELIEF SECTIONS

37. Once the base slab has been completely smoothed and leveled, position the plastic template on the backsplash and countertop in preparation for tracing the lines of the relief design.

37

38. Compare the original drawing to the plastic template to determine if the template is correctly positioned.

39. Trace the design onto the slab by pressing the plastic into the clay with a rounded chopstick.

40. Once the entire design has been traced onto the clay, peel the template away to reveal the lines of the design indented in the clay.

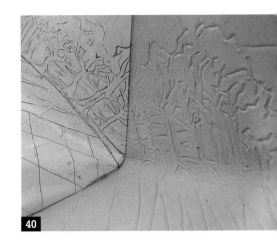

41. Retrace the lines in the clay with a chopstick. Begin to establish areas of relief by applying thin layers of rolled clay to the surface, in patches which can be manipulated with your fingers by tearing, cutting, or pinching. (See section on layering and cutting on page 33.)

42. Add textural lines, such as cross-hatched areas, with the end of a chopstick.

43. To build up curved relief forms that represent the trunks of the trees, first score the outlines of the trees in preparation for receiving small patches of rolled clay.

44. Pinch a small patch of clay together with your fingertips to build up a relief texture.

45. Apply this clay to form a tree's trunk and continue to shape it once it is placed on the slab.

46. Use a sponge to press any added relief to the base slab and insure that it won't come off during firing.

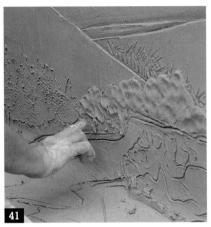

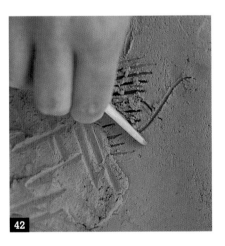

44

47. Continue to draw and enhance elements of the design, build three-dimensional shapes, add texture, and refine areas until the design takes shape in the clay. The process of drawing and building this design is guided by a drawing while being open to improvisational additions or subtractions. The beauty of working in clay is that it can be changed during the process of implementing an idea.

48. Press leaves into the clay to add another textural design to the base slab.

49. Scrape and draw lines to represent flowing water using your fingers, a scraper, and a chopstick at the edge of the sink's cutout.

SECTIONING THE COUNTERTOP

50. Cut through the lines indicating the sink cutout to the surface of the worktable.

51. Cut a semi-circular notch out of one edge of the sink to make removing the clay section easier.

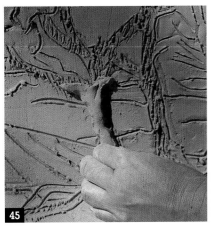

45

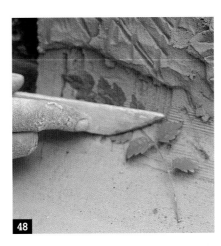

48

46

49

50

51

47

52. Fold up and remove the clay.

53. The countertop and backsplash are now ready for trimming and sectioning.

54. Since a project of this sort can take several days to complete in the wet clay, spray the clay lightly with water before placing plastic over it at night to prevent it from drying out too rapidly.

55. Begin work again by using a needle tool to trim the top edge of the backsplash at the top of the backboard.

56,57. Draw preliminary grooves in the clay with a chopstick to find the best configuration for sectioning the piece (see page 35 for suggestions on sectioning). If you make a mistake or change your mind about where to make a cut, these grooves can be easily erased.

58. Cut the lines of the sections through to the work surface using a knife, needle tool, or other sharp tool.

59. Allow the clay to dry and shrink while still on the work surface until it is leather hard. At this point of dryness, remove the vertical backsplash sections and place them on a separate table to dry. When all of the sections are bone dry, they're ready to be glazed.

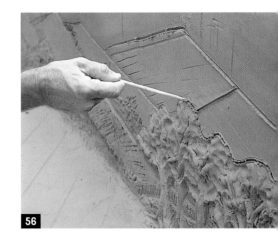

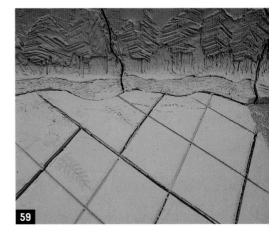

INSTALLING THE COUNTERTOP

This installation system is the one that we most commonly use at Stonehaus. Using felt and expanded wire lath embedded with mortar creates an interface between a drywall or plywood substrate that is substantial and waterproof. This versatile setting system can be used in so many different situations that you'll probably find yourself using it more than any other installation method.

1. Use a carpenter's flat bar and long screwdriver to pry the old tile countertop (including tile, mortar, and wire) off of its plywood substrate.

2. Nail a layer of tar paper or organic felt followed by a layer of expanded wire lath over the exposed plywood substrate. Use a ⅜-inch notched trowel to spread the wire lath with a coat of thinset mortar.

3. Using a margin trowel, "back-butter" sections of the ceramic countertop with additional thinset, especially sections that are warped. This process improves the contact between them and the setting surface.

4. Use the numbers that you carved into the sections along with a map of the piece for reference when assembling the puzzle-like pieces of the countertop.

5. When adding the sections, work from the center out, especially if the project has a corner. Doing this will increase your chances of making all the pieces key successfully.

6,7. Since part of the countertop needs to be set to a masonry wall, coat the surface with latex admixture and set directly to the surface for this portion.

8. To set the cap tile to its vertical edge, heavily "backbutter" it with thinset and embed it directly into the wire lath. Doing this will avoid the mess caused by mortar dripping off the vertical surface.

9. Use duct tape to hold edge tile in place until the mortar has set.

10,11. Mix grout to the consistency of cake batter. Pile it onto the surface of the tile, and work it into the joints with a gloved hand.

12,13. Repeatedly wipe the grout with a clean sponge until it is evenly distributed in the joints and the tiles are clean.

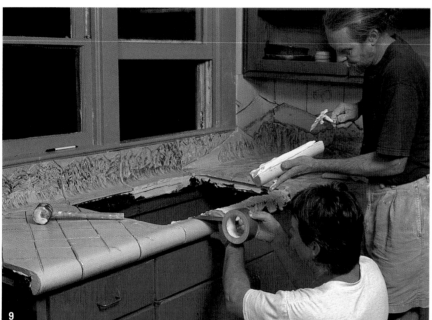

BUILDING DOOR SURROUNDS

Doors are an important architectural feature because they are passageways into a different architectural space. Since people are forced to pause before entering them, they provide an opportunity for artistic embellishment.

When planning a ceramic door surround, you should consider the following:

1. The type of surface that you'll be installing on will require different installation procedures (see chapter four for more information). If it is brick, concrete, or stone, an installation that uses an interface will be the most suitable if you're doing one that isn't permanent. If it is a wood surface, you can use screws to fasten sections directly to the building. For a permanent installation, set the piece to the building with thinset mortar.

2. If the doorway is inset, you'll have to decide how to treat the space between the face of the building and the door jamb. This space can be left bare, tiled, or wrapped with a return (see the project that follows for an example of a door surround return).

3. Make note of any features that might restrict the dimensions of your design, such as light fixtures, windows, walls, or roof overhangs.

Starting at the lower left on page 76 and continuing clockwise on page 77:

KATHRYN ALLEN (Seattle, Washington), *Mayan Gateway*, door surround, 1995; 84 x 80 x 4 in. (210 x 200 x 10 cm); stoneware; slab-built, decorative elements added; red iron oxide wash applied and sanded; Δ6. Photo by Tom Holt

PETER KING (Pensacola, Florida), *Tudor*, 9 ft. 7½ in. (2.9 m), 1995; unglazed stoneware, tile pressed and slab built; Δ5-6.

PETER KING (Pensacola, Florida), *Gaudi*, 12 x 6 ft. (3.6 x 1.8 m), 1998; unglazed terra cotta stoneware, handbuilt, slab built; Δ5-6.

ANGELLA POZO (Cleveland, Ohio), *Pines Portal*, Penland School of Crafts, Penland, North Carolina, 1994; 10 x 6¼ x 6 ft. (3 x 1.9 x 1.8 m); terra cotta, imbedded copper wire; slab-rolled and handcut tiles, relief and coil-built mosaics; Δ04. Photo by Dana Moore

DIANA AND TOM WATSON (Hermosa Beach, California), *untitled*, entryway for residence, 1998; 92 x 54 x 6 in. (230 x 135 x 15 cm); tiles, 4 x 4 in. (10 x 10 cm) and 6 x 6 in. (15 x 15 cm); earthenware; cuerda seca technique; Δ05. Photo by Dana L. Walker

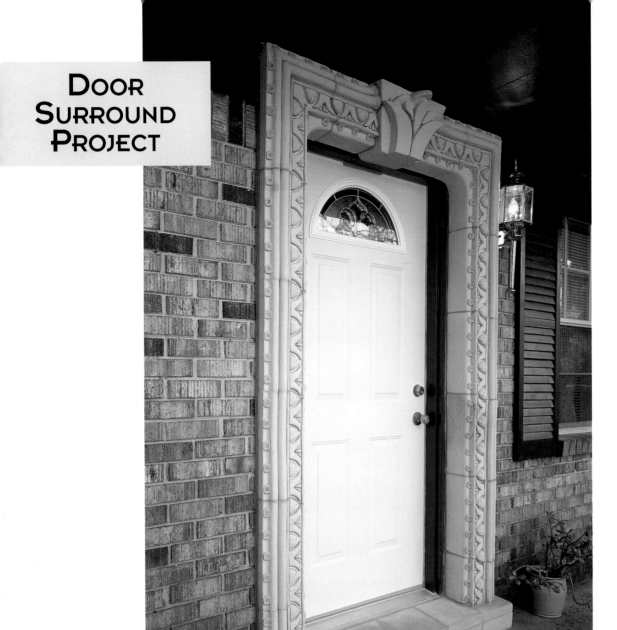

This door surround was designed for my brother John who is an avid sports fisherman. I designed the tile molding and keystone with stylized fish heads and tails as references to a traditional form of molding known as "egg and dart." The measurements accomodate a door which has an 83-inch-high by 40-inch-wide opening. The face of the surround is 8 inches wide, and the wrap is 4 inches deep.

To make such a door surround, you'll build a base slab, make molding with a draw tool, make tiles for molding with an adapted hydraulic press, and box-build a keystone. All of these techniques have been covered in chapter two, and you can refer back to sections for more information if needed.

LAYING THE BASE SLAB

1. After arranging work tables in a formation that will accomodate the base slab of the door surround, measure and mark off the outside perimeter lines of the surround by using a carpenter's chalk line to snap a line. Extend the chalk lines beyond their intersecting points so that they will be visible after you lay the untrimmed base slab.

2, 3. Trail a cup of grog onto the work surface and spread a thin layer within the perimeter lines. The grog will keep the clay from sticking to the surface and allow it to move while drying.

4. Once the grog is spread over the work surface, and the perimeter lines are clearly visible, it is ready to receive the slabs.

5. Roll out a slab of a size that you can handle for beginning the process of building the base slab. Carry the slab to the work surface on its canvas backing.

6. Use the canvas backing to flip the slab onto the table, allowing it to overlap the edge of the work table so that it can be used to form the inner wrap of the surround.

7. Peel away the canvas, and press the slab into place to form the wrap of the surround.

8. Overlap the next slab by

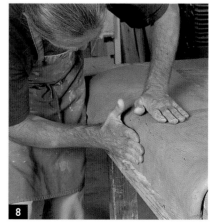

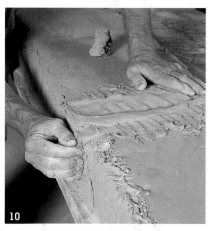

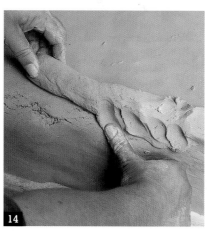

a couple of inches on top of the first one, and continue to join slabs to complete the base slab.

9-13. Pound, scrape, and smooth the seams to make a single unified slab using your fist, fingers, and trowels as needed.

14. Use a medium-sized coil of clay to reinforce the outside corner of the surround where the clay drapes over the edge. Don't use slip to apply the coil or this additional clay will pull loose during the draw process.

15. After you've overlapped all slabs and pounded, smoothed, and reinforced the seams, shape the edge with a rounded draw tool, echoing the curve that you want for the corner of the surround.

16, 17. Using the extended chalk lines as a reference, lay a straight edge, such as a strip of aluminum flat stock or wood, along the line that forms the outside edge of the surround. Trim the edge with a needle tool.

18. The resulting base slab forms the foundation of the surround on which to build the other three-dimensional components.

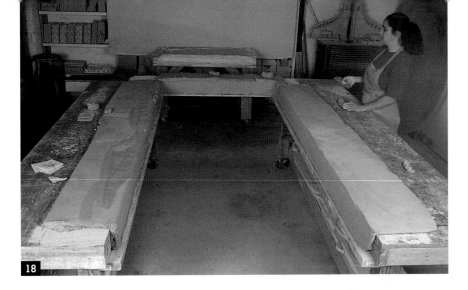

USING A DRAW TOOL TO MAKE A MOLDING

These particular drawn moldings are designed with two sets of symmetrical arches that face one another. The strips used on the edge of the surround are formed by cutting the arched molding in half after it has stiffened on the draw board.

19, 20. Begin by placing an appropriately-sized draw board on a work table long enough to accomodate the length of molding needed. Roll slabs of slightly over half the thickness of the final molding as dictated by the profile of the draw tool. (Because of the draw's arched profile, a narrower slab will be added later on top of this slab to reduce the amount of clay that needs to be removed from the sides and make drawing easier.) Overlap the slabs so that the seams can be joined.

21, 22. Pound and scrape the seams of the slabs.

23. Cut away the excess clay from the slab along the edge of the draw board using a knife, needle tool, or ice pick.

24. Use a needle tool or comb to score the center of the clay in preparation for receiving a narrower slab of clay.

25, 26. Cut away excess clay with a miter tool to form an angle which will conform to the draw tool. Removing this excess clay will make it possible to draw the tool smoothly down the draw board.

27. Add a slab of clay wide enough and high enough to fill

the rest of the profile of the draw tool on top of this slab.

28, 29. Press the slab into place and drizzle water over the surface with a sponge to lubricate it in preparation for using the draw tool.

30. Place the draw tool at the end of the board opposite the draw tab that is affixed to the

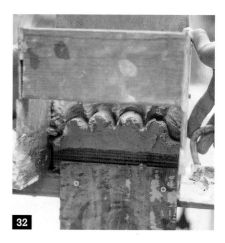

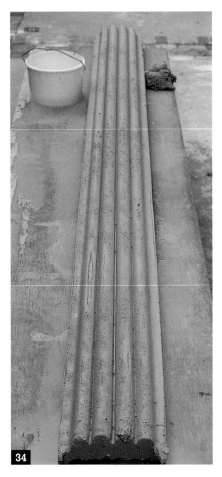

table to hold the board in place. Slowly and evenly draw the tool over the clay with a slight downward pressure to remove the excess and form the molding's profile.

31. Make several passes with the draw tool, sprinkling water over the surface prior to each pass until the clay takes the form of the draw tool.

32. At the end of each pass, you'll notice the build-up of excess clay on the draw.

33. Fill any tears with soft clay and pass the draw tool over the surface once more to eliminate excess clay.

34. The molding is now ready to dry on the draw board before being moved to the base slab of the surround.

35. As soon as the draw is finished, cut the molding from the draw board with a cutting wire and leave it on the board for transporting.

36. After making another strip of molding (half of which will be used to trim the top of the door), leave the two strips to dry overnight or long enough that the clay can be handled without causing it to distort.

37. Move the molding on its board onto the work surface next to the surround's trimmed edge. Use a knife to slice the molding in half to form two symmetrical strips that will be placed on either side of the door.

38, 39. Determine the placement of the molding on the base slab by measuring in from the edge the width of the molding. Cut rectagular holes in the base slab within this width to remove some of the clay and reduce the overall weight and thickness of the surround.

40. In order to prepare for eventual addition of another section of relief tile (see steps 54-68), mark off the width of the tile adjacent to the molding. Cut an additional row of holes in the clay in preparation for adding the tile later. Score and slip the outermost area of the base slab to receive the first set of molding strips.

41. To remove the molding from the draw board, turn the board on its side. Place a straight edge, such as a long board or aluminum strip, underneath the side of the molding so that it can be balanced on top of it.

42. Lift the molding on the straight edge, and move it to the base slab.

43. Align the edge of the strip with the line that indicates the inside edge of the molding. Tilt the molding into place. Since the area was painted with slip earlier, it is easy to adjust the molding by sliding it into place.

44. Sew the molding to the base slab with a needle tool by making zigzag cuts along the seam.

45. Miter the upper right corner of the molding by using two framing squares placed upright and a cutting wire to create a 45-degree angle.

46. To miter the connecting top section of molding, turn it vertically and position two 45-degree

angle squares on either side. Use a cutting wire to cut an angle that will butt against the top edge of the molding that has already been cut.

47. Move the molding into its approximate place while on the straight edge.

48. Flip and slide it into place so that the two angles can be joined to form the upper right corner of the surround. Continue the process of applying the outside molding by mitering the other end of the top section before adding strips down the left side of the surround.

49. Cut ⅝-inch-wide strips of ½-inch-thick slab to use for back-filling the seams created between the molding and the base slab. (These dimensions don't have to be exact, but these strips are of a convenient size to use for this purpose.)

50. Press the strips into place along the seams.

51. Use the unnotched edge of a square trowel to remove the excess clay used for filling the seams and to smooth the joining edges of the molding and the base slab.

52. Join the seams between molding strips by "sewing" them and filling them with soft clay.

53. Use a draw tool cut to

mimic the profile of the molding to smooth it where the seams were joined.

51

48

52

46

49

47

50

53

54

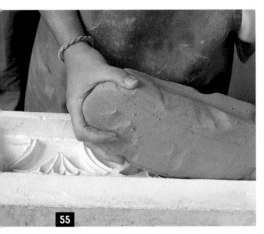

55

56

57

MAKING PRESSED TILE MOLDING USING A HYDRAULIC TILE PRESS

This section shows how to make another form of more intricately patterned molding using the tile press described on pages 15 and 16. This molding can be made on the same day as the drawn molding described in the previous section to provide a similar drying time for both sets of molding.

54. Use a sieve to sprinkle the cast plaster mold with a drying agent such as talc, cornstarch, silica, or clay.

55. Wedge a lump of clay into an elogated block and drop it into the mold.

56. Since a high relief mold is being used in this example, first press the clay into the mold by hand into the deepest parts of the relief. Doing this will assure that all of the detail of the mold appears on the pressed clay form.

57. Place the clay-filled mold under the hydraulic press and compress it by extending the hydraulic cylinder. Creating a nicely formed tile takes practice—too little pressure will result in an incompletely formed tile while too much pressure can

58

59

60

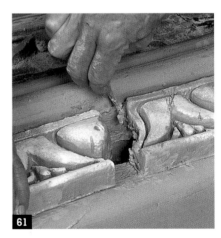

61

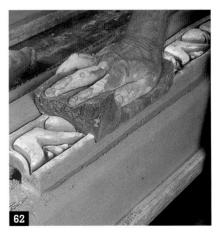

62

63

64

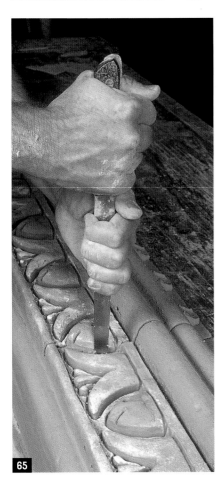

65

break the plaster mold. (To protect the mold we often place rubber matting between the plaster mold and the bottom metal base plate.)

58. After pressing the mold, release the pressure, and allow the springs on the press to raise the top press plate, the mold, and the clay form slightly above the pressing surface. Pry the mold from the top plate using a long screwdriver. Remove the plaster mold from the press, and pull out the press board with the tile attached before flipping it over on your work surface.

59. Create a clean line for the bottom of the tile by using a cutting wire to slice the tile away from the excess clay.

60. Prepare the surface of the base slab for receiving the molding by scoring and slipping the area where it will be placed alongside the drawn molding (see step 40). After the surface is prepared, miter the ends of two sections of molding to form the upper right corner.

61. Add the sections of pressed tile, which are designed to key together, to create the inside decorative molding. Make a small mark with a needle tool on the side of the adjacent molding where each joins the other. The finished door surround will be sectioned along the breaks between the sections.

62. Press the sprigged form into place with a stiff sponge.

63. After placing all of the molding sections, section the piece using a framing square and needle tool to indicate the initial sectioning lines.

64, 65. As if you're cutting pieces of cake, use a knife to carve straight through the relief to the work surface. The pieces cut will reflect the lines of the

keyed sections of molding which were added inside the drawn molding sections.

66. Cut decorative square buttons out of clay and place them at consistent intervals, several inches apart, around the perimeter of the surround.

67. Use a clay or plaster stamp to press them into place.

68. Use the blunt end of a needle tool to add holes in the center of these squares; that will be used later for holding screws when you install the surround.

66

67

68

Box Building the Keystone

The keystone, or the focal point of the surround's decoration at the top center of the door, mimics a traditional stone feature that served the function of locking other stones together. This keystone is built directly on the base slab after trimming away a section of molding at the top to accomodate it.

69. To box build the keystone, begin by using a straight edge to cut away molding from the top center of the surround to leave the keystone's outside dimension on the base slab. Score one inch within the perimeter of the keystone shape in preparation for adding the side walls. Score a one-inch line down the center of the wedge shape for receiving the bracing wall. Cut holes in the base slab between the lines that have

been scored. Cut side walls according to dimensions and stand them up. (These can be tapered by trimming with a needle tool or wire once they're in place, or they can be cut to their exact dimensions before standing them up.) Sew the seams together. Add a bracing slab down the center. Cut the facing slab slightly larger than needed and lay it on top of the side and bracing walls. Trim it to the dimension of the wedge shape. Cut the decorative, rounded sections of relief slab that form the fishtail-shaped emblem on top of the facing slab. Score and slip the areas to receive these sections and apply them.

70, 71. After the door surround is completed, cover the surround with plastic for drying. Doing this will allow the moisture to seep from section to section and assist in fusing the clay of various sections together.

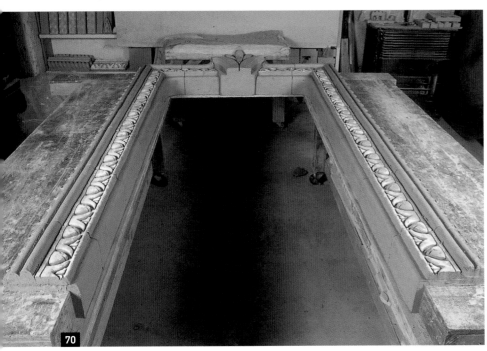

INSTALLING THE DOOR SURROUND

To mechanically fasten a door surround, it usually makes the job easier if you create a plywood interface between the ceramic sections and the substrate. The plywood provides a consistent flat surface into which sections can be screwed. This system works well over wallboard, brick, block, stucco, or siding. It can also be used for temporary gallery or museum installations. For this particular door surround, we used a layer of sealed weather-resistant plywood known as "sign board."

1, 2. Cut a ¾-inch-thick plywood strip to the width of the surround. Hold the strip in place along the door's edge. Use a hammer drill to make two 3-inch-deep pilot holes through the plywood into the masonry on either side of the strip near its center. (A hammer drill makes drilling into stone, brick, or concrete much easier.)

3. Drill 3-inch self-tapping concrete screws through the pilot holes to hold the board in place. Make certain that the board is correctly aligned with the door at this point.

4. Working your way up the door, insert screws along either edge of the wood approximately two feet apart along its length. When you finish, the board should be flush with the masonry, and the plywood should be attached near both of its edges.

5. Place the bottom ceramic section of the surround on the plywood, and drill 2-inch drywall screws through two of the screw holes to hold it. (The screws should be long enough that they reach through the ceramic section and into the width of the plywood without hitting the masonry substrate.) Do not place all of the screws at this point. Assemble the entire surround first with as few screws as possible, so that adjustments can be made later if necessary without having to remove a lot of screws.

6-8. Continue to stack sections and fasten them for the purpose of correct placement.

9-12. Because of its higher relief, the keystone requires longer screws to hold it in place. After screwing it in place above the door, the installation can be assessed to make certain that all sections are properly aligned.

13, 14. Once you're satisfied with the placement of all the sections, add the missing screws to the surround for the permanent assemblage of the piece.

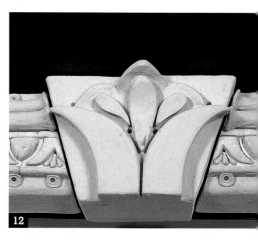

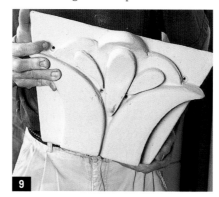

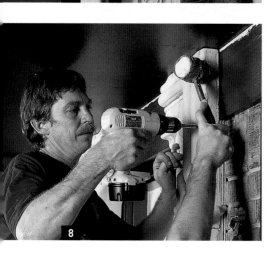

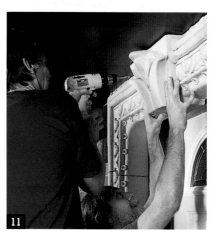

BUILDING FIREPLACE SURROUNDS

Fireplaces hold deep symbolic connections for the human psyche. When humans first began using fire in the most rudimentary ways, it became the center of tribal and family life. Eventually, fireplaces provided a source of light, heat, food, and security. In Spanish, *hogar* means fireplace, home, and family.

With the introduction of modern heating, fireplaces faded in importance as a main heat source. By the 1970s, they became popular again as a major point of aesthetic interest in the home.

Measuring for a Fireplace Surround

A ceramic fireplace surround can form a major point of emphasis in a home or room. Ceramic sections can be installed over an existing fireplace or the walls surrounding a metal insert fireplace. To design a surround, you must consider the following: the size of the wall or existing surround around the firebox, and its relationship to the opening; whether the fireplace has a raised hearth or one that is flush with the floor; and the width and height of the fireplace opening. If you are

Above: **PETER KING** (Pensacola, Florida), *Nautilus*, 10 x 8 ft. (3 x 2.4 m), 1995; glazed stoneware, handbuilt; Δ5-6.

Below: **JAN EDWARDS** (Portland, Oregon), *untitled*, fireplace surround for Portland Audubon Society, 1996; 49¼ x 75⅞ x ½ in. (1.2 x 1.9m x 1.3 cm); terra cotta; hand-cut tiles decorated with painting, sgraffito, stamping, sponging; Δ05. Photo by Ed Gowans

making the hearth, remember to deduct the thickness of the hearth tile from the dimensions of the fireplace surround.

If you're covering a conventional brick or stone fireplace, the dimensions that you have to work with are already established (such as the size of the opening, which is established by the firebox). Metal insert fireplaces require additional considerations that are discussed in the next section.

Metal Fireplaces

With the introduction of the metal fireplace unit during the 1970s, fireplaces became affordable for almost any home. You'll find that most new constructions have metal fireplaces rather than masonry ones.

Metal fireplaces have become an industry standard. They are composed of self-contained inserts that can be housed in a wooden frame, easily installed in any type of construction, and added to the upper floors of a building without additional structural reinforcement. They are functional and efficient, but lack visual interest. Since many people still want their fireplace to contribute to the architectural design of their home, the unadorned metal insert fireplace lends a great opportunity to the architectural ceramicist.

When beginning a commission for a fireplace surround to be installed around a metal fireplace unit, obtain as much available technical data as you can. Talk to the distributor, explain your project, and ask if there are any special considerations that might be important for you to know. Most metal insert fireplaces are safe to frame around with no risk of combustion. When designing the surround,

Top: **W. MITCH YUNG** (Branson, Missouri), *untitled,* fireplace, 1997; 72 x 96 in. (1.8 x 2.4 m); red earthenware; handbuilt, slab construction, bas-relief carving; terra sigillata; Δ04. Photo by Rockafellow Photography

Above: **PETER KING** (Pensacola, Florida), *Gotham,* 7 ft. 1 in. x 4 ft. 8 in. (2.1 x 1.4 m), 1992; glazed stoneware; Δ6.

you'll have to decide beforehand how much of the metal insert to cover and how to cover it. (For Stonehaus commissions, we generally cover as much of the insert as we can without interfering with its function.)

Metal fireplaces are often designed with an enclosed circulation system with front vents. Don't cover these or cap them off unless you use a *cowling*, or a hooded section that is open to allow air to circulate through the vents. The size of this opening should approximate the surface area of the vent itself so the airflow is not restricted.

FIREPLACE CURTAINS AND DOORS

On metal fireplace units with chain mail curtains, there are small areas on either side of the fireplace opening that house the curtains when they're open. Make the hole of the ceramic surround the same size as the firebox, and you'll automatically cover these curtains once they're open.

If the fireplace has bi-folding, hinged glass doors, it is usually necessary to enlarge the opening to a size that is wider than the doors in order to accommodate them in an open position. Some people may want the option of adding doors later, so it's important to ask your client about his preferences before planning the specifics of your design.

Above: **TERRY NICHOLAS** (Ponte Vedra Beach, Florida), *Various Creatures*, fireplace surround, 1997; 38 x 42 in. (95 x 105 cm); terra cotta and white earthenware; carved tiles, press molded, slab-built, textured and carved; ∆05. Photo by David Porter

Right: **LISA BREZNAK** (Peekskill, New York), *untitled*, fireplace; 1997; 40 x 44 x 2¾ in. (100 x 110 x 6.9 cm); medallion, 16 x 19 in. (40 x 47.5 cm); tiles, 5¾ x 5¾ in. (14.4 x 14.4 cm); white earthenware; slab medallion, hand-molded tiles, incised details; ∆04. Photo by Howard Goodman

FIREPLACE SURROUND PROJECT

This surround was designed by Stonehaus for interior designer Ann Cramer with whom I have collaborated on numerous projects. She gave me latitude to come up with a design, and suggested that she didn't mind if the square opening of her present fireplace was altered. The design is dictated largely by the oval opening that we created. The piece was influenced by Spanish art nouveau, pre-Columbian art, and contemporary chaos theory.

This piece employs most of the techniques that you've already read about and seen in chapter two, and in the making of the countertop and door surround in chapter three. These include laying a base slab, building a column, box building a form, building a free-form construction, and using a draw tool.

LAYING THE BASE SLAB

1. Cut two strips of ⅛-inch luan plywood that are the length of the circumference of the fireplace's opening. These strips will be overlapped to form an inside ledge in the opening. (The hole is cut to the dimension of the fireplace's opening in a piece of plywood which rests on top of the center opening between three tables set in a U-shape.)

2. Bend the first luan strip gently so that it fits into the precut hole.

3. Use screws or nails and staples to affix the strip to the edge of the plywood. Overlap a second strip for support and affix in the same manner.

4. Mark the fireplace surround's perimeter lines by snapping a carpenter's chalk line. Use a sketch with dimensions mapped out as a guide. Don't forget to add the clay's shrinkage.

5. Spread a layer of grog within the perimeter lines.

6. Roll large slabs to surround the fireplace opening, and allow the edge of the slab to drop into the fireplace opening to form an inside edge. Continue adding slabs around the opening which cover the outside perimeter of the fireplace. Overlap them roughly twice the thickness of the slab to join them. (Here they're overlapped 2 inches because we're using a 1-inch-thick slab.)

7. Pound the seams together with your fists, and press the clay into place with your fingers. Use your fingers to press and smooth the inside edge of the fireplace into place.

8. Add clay to any unlevel areas between seams. Rake and smooth the clay with your fingertips to achieve a level surface. Use trowels, scrapers, and rollers to finish smoothing the slab.

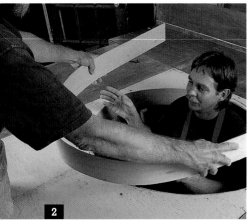

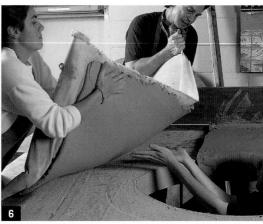

9. Attach a backboard to the table with screws and clamps. The backboard should project upward the width of the mantel. Roll slabs that are slightly wider than the backboard, and lap them over the edge to form the mantel slab.

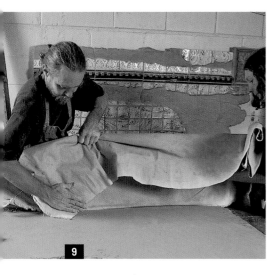

10. Join the seam between the face of the surround and the mantel slab by pounding the seams with the outside edge of your hand.

11. Repeat this process, adding slabs and overlapping their seams, until you've formed the length of the mantel.

Building a Spiral Column

12. Build a draped column using PVC pipe as described on pages 28-30. Mark off and score the lines indicating the area to receive the inside edges of the column. Set the draped column on its PVC pipe support in place on the base slab.

13. Remove the PVC pipe and "sew" the column's outside edges to the base slab.

14. Make a few passes with a hand-held draw tool cut to conform to the column's final shape, and form a smooth, uniform column. Do not use

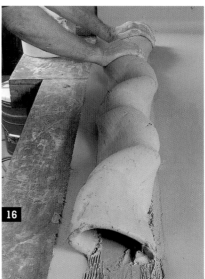

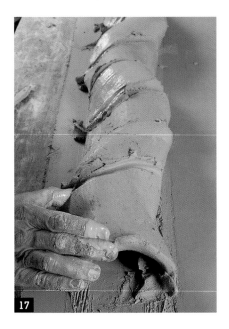

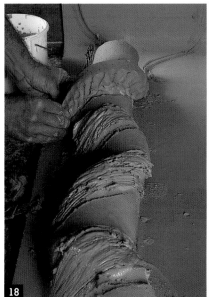

water for this draw. The tool will both smooth and compress the clay.

15. Grab two adjacent sections of the column and twist them in opposite directions to distort the clay into a spiraling column.

16. Continue to twist and distort the column until you reach the top of it.

17. Mark off lines indicating an enhanced spiral on the column.

18. Score and slip these lines, and add strips of clay to the surface to build up the profile of the spiral.

19. Scrape and join these slabs together using your fingertips to round and shape the clay.

20. Add an additional slab at the base of this column, and shape it by hand to form a flaring pediment.

21. Brace the hollow area underneath the pediment with a small column of rolled clay that forms a supporting tree-like shape. (The capital that tops the column will be added later during the finishing of the mantel. See steps 64-67.)

BUILDING A BOX COLUMN

22. Mark off the perimeter of the box column, and score the base slab along lines where standing slabs will be added. Cut holes in the slab with a piece of drainpipe or needle tool to lighten the form and allow air to escape after the form has been enclosed.

23. Insert a slightly narrower dowel into the drainpipe to push out the clay that is removed to make the holes.

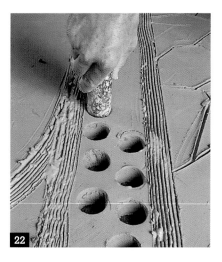

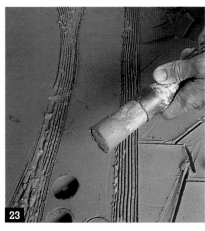

24, 25. Begin by building the tapered rectangular form. (The curved side portions will be added later.) Stand up the left wall along the line that has been drawn in the base slab. (Notice that the side walls taper slightly as they descend to the base of the surround.)

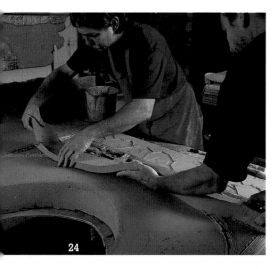

24

25

26

26. Add the right wall and the end slabs to form a rectangle, aligning them with the lines drawn in the base slab. "Sew" the walls to the base slab and smooth the seams.

27. Add bracing slabs at intervals of 6 inches to connect the side walls and support the facing slab.

28. Cut a facing slab that conforms to the perimeter of the rectangular form. Score and slip the top edges of the standing walls. Score the outside edges of the facing slab. Gently flip the slab into position on top of the standing walls, and make marks on the outside walls indicating the position of the braces (see next photo).

29. "Sew" the joining seams between the facing slab and side walls.

30. Reinforce the seams with strips of clay, and smooth the sides until they are level.

31. Fuse the facing slab to the walls by pounding them together

27

using a flat board and a rubber mallet. Doing this also helps to flatten out any irregularities.

32. Check the measurement of the height of the walls of the rectangular form in preparation for cutting and building additional walls. These walls will form the arched sections that echo the curve of the fireplace opening.

33. Cut a long piece of slab to be used making the curved forms.

28

29

30

34. Within the perimeter of the drawn lines, cut out holes with a needle tool in the side of the rectangular form. (Like the holes in a cement block, this subtraction of weight will lighten the overall form.) Score the edges of the walls in preparation for adding additional walls.

35. Stand up a wall that extends to the end of the top drawn line.

36. "Sew" the wall where it joins the rectangular form and the base slab.

37. Stand up a curved wall that matches the perimeter line drawn in the base slab.

38. Rake the areas where the slab joins the standing wall of the rectangular form, and smooth it to make a continuous curved wall.

39. To make sizing the top facing slab simpler, cut a slab that is slightly larger than necessary and echoes the shape of the curved form. Flip it into place on top of the walls. Trim it by running a needle tool underneath it along the line of the standing walls.

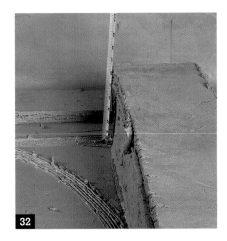

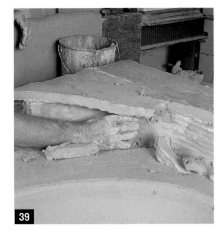

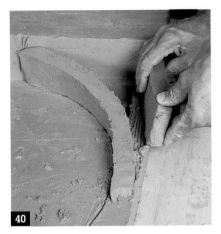

40. Add another curved form at the base of the rectangular column, repeating the process used for the top curved form. Smooth and finish the curved additions to the column.

41. To create an interesting surface effect on the column after it is built, gauge holes between the inside braces in the surface to create hollow sculptural spaces. Enhance and strengthen the edges of the openings by reinforcing them with strips or coils of clay.

42. Hand build high-relief accents out of blocks of clay by shaping them before pounding them with a stick into crystal-like forms.

43. Drive the ends of these pointed forms into the soft walls of the right side of the column.

FINISHING THE OVAL OPENING

44. Reinforce the opening with additional clay strips that are wide enough to cover the opening from the outside to the inside edge.

45. Press these additional strips into place.

46. Blend them with the base slab by using your fingers to smooth the seams where the strip joins the base slab.

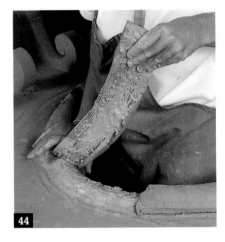

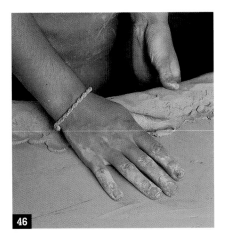

46

50

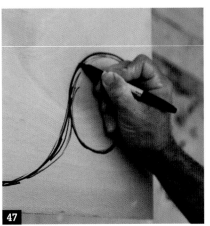

47

48

49

ADDING THE MANTEL BRACKETS

47, 48. Draw a template for a mantel bracket on a square of luan plywood. Cut the template with a jigsaw or sharp razor knife. (This decorative bracket mimics the organic curves of the fireplace's other features.) Cut an identical template so that you have two to use together later.

49. Add long coils of clay to the corner where the mantel meets the base slab. Then use a round rib to smooth the clay and form a slightly curved corner. Doing this strengthens the corner both visually and physically.

50. Smooth the surface before marking off the placement of the brackets.

51. Draw a line along the top of the mantel to indicate where it will be cut later. Mark off the placement of the brackets using a framing square, and score and slip the lines.

52. Use the bracket template as a pattern to cut out forms in a slab that are slightly larger than the template. (An ice pick works well as a substitute needle tool.) The brackets will be trimmed later.

53. Score and slip the facing edges of the brackets, and stand them up on the scored and slipped paths on the base slab. Thoroughly "sew" the brackets into place, and fill the

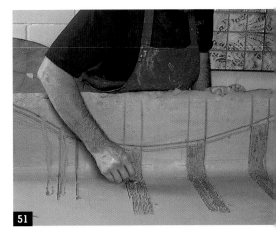

51

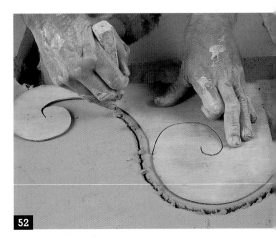

52

53

54.

seams with strips of soft clay for reinforcement. Clean up the seams by scraping them with a square-edged piece of vinyl or luan, or a potter's rib.

54. Cut out the pieces of slab along the curved line of the mantel between the brackets and remove them.

55. Once they're all in place,

check the position of the brackets from various angles and make certain that they're straight.

56, 57. Place the two luan templates on either side of the clay bracket. Make certain that they are firmly seated against the base slab and the mantel.

58-60. Use a potter's cutting wire to trim away the excess

55.

57.

58.

60.

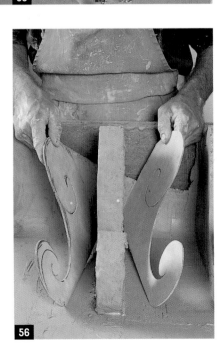

56.

59.

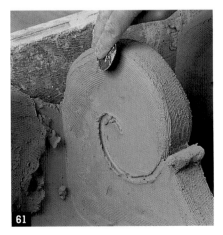

61.

clay by running the wire firmly along the profile of the templates. By cutting the profiles after they are in place, the brackets come out cleaner with fewer distortions.

61. Finish the edges of the brackets by removing excess clay and smoothing them with a scraper and rubber rib until they are consistently rounded.

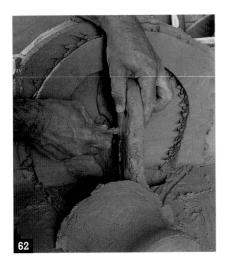

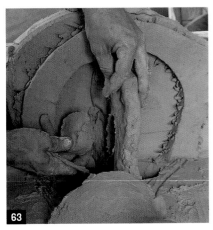

ADDING A CAPITAL TO THE SPIRAL COLUMN

62, 63. Now that the mantel backboard is shaped and the brackets added, you can add a capital to the previously constructed spiral column. This capital conforms to the shape of the mantel where the two join. To build this free-form construction, add a circle of clay and "sew" it to the mantel. Within this circle, attach a center brace reflecting the finished shape of the capital. Cut a hole in the brace and remove the clay to lighten it.

64. Add two more radiating braces and join them at the top to form a bridge to the clay circle added earlier to the mantel. These braces will support the facing slab, so don't forget to subtract its width from the braces when cutting them.

65. Cover the braces with a slab cut roughly to a size that will wrap from one side of the capital to the other.

66. Manipulate the facing slab with your fingers until you've achieved the free-form shape that you want.

67. Smooth the entire capital and column with a flexible rib or a piece of vinyl siding.

Removing the Mantel

68, 69. Slide a long knife behind the mantel to loosen it from the backboard before removing it. Fill and smooth the top side of the mantel.

70. Add a slab of clay to the edge and top of the mantel to give it a more substantial appearance.

Adding a Free-Form Construction

71. To make a sweeping form that connects the fireplace's opening with the base of the spiral column, begin by carving a portion of the edge of the opening. Draw lines in the clay to indicate the rough placement of the rest of the form.

72. Hand cut doughnut-shaped braces. The shape of these braces allow air to pass from one chamber to another.

73, 74. Place braces along the areas to be covered with facing slabs. (The smaller set of braces that sits next to the larger ones will be used to form a complementary form beside the larger one.)

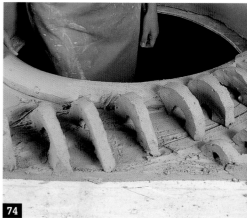

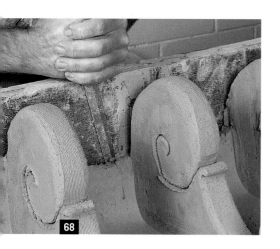

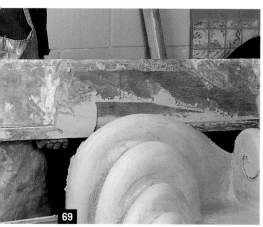

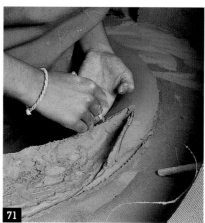

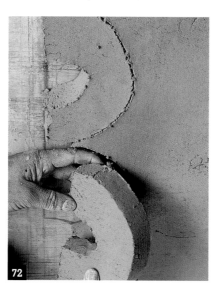

75. Use a piece of drainpipe to cut holes in the base slab between the braces.

76. Cut a facing slab to cover the braces. Score and slip the edges of the braces and the back of the facing slab.

77. Conform the facing slab to the braces, smoothing it with your fingers. "Sew" the slab to the base slab.

78. Pull a tape measure from the base slab over the top of the form and down to find the width of the next facing slab that you cut.

79. Once all of the braces are covered, scrape and smooth the entire surface, adding and subtracting clay if needed during the process.

80. Draw rough lines in the clay with the blunt end of a needle tool or a chopstick to indicate where the piece will be sectioned. Try to plan cuts halfway between braces when possible to keep the sections from drooping.

81. Cut the sections with a long knife and a decisive movement.

82. Leave the finished piece to dry for several days before glazing and firing.

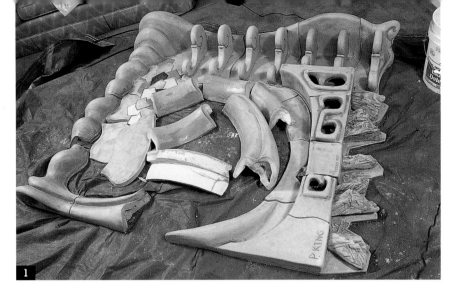

INSTALLING THE FIREPLACE SURROUND

This project provided us with an ideal substrate for a permanent installation—a red brick fireplace facade. Before beginning the installation, we enlisted a professional to cover the existing brick with a smooth coat of fresh cement.

Because the original shape of the fireplace was square, we added brick sections around an oval form to alter the opening. The supporting form is made out of a ¾-inch luan top wrapped with a strip of 1/8-inch luan. It is slightly smaller (about 9 percent) than the oval opening used to build the surround in wet clay, to provide room for a layer of thinset. Using the form to prop bricks and mortar, an oval substrate was created by adding trimmed bricks. To make the mortar fire resistant, 30 percent fireclay was added to it. Use the following steps to install a similar piece.

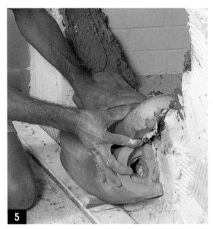

1. Lay out the fireplace surround on the floor near the installation site.

2. Once the mortar has set around the added bricks, remove the oval luan form.

3. Apply thinset with a ⅜-inch notched trowel to an area that you can set within 20 minutes, because the mortar will begin to form a thin skin on top.

4. Position the first piece by centering it under the bottom of the oval opening.

5. Position the second piece using registration marks cut into the edges of each piece as a guide. Place a small wooden shim underneath the edge of the piece to hold it in place above the hearth.

6. Embed the pieces in the mortar by striking them several times with a rubber mallet.

7. "Backbutter" each section that you add as you move from the bottom of the installation up.

8. Strike the newly added sections with a mallet.

9. As efficiently as possible, add pieces around the opening. You have about 20 minutes during which you can slide pieces to adjust their position without breaking the mortar bed.

10, 11. Fill holes in the back of high relief sections with thinset to create cement "pegs" which will further increase the strength of the bond once the pieces have set.

12. Rake the mortared surface of the sections smooth with a ⅜-inch notched trowel.

13. The piece is now about half set, and wooden shims have been placed underneath the

lower sections to hold them in place.

14. Use a map made when the fireplace was sectioned to reassemble one of the more detailed sections of the surround.

15. After placing the small pieces on the upper left side, proceed to the top of the circular arch.

16. Set the last three pieces of the arch simultaneously so that they can be properly keyed together.

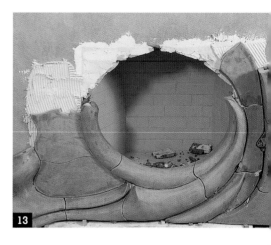

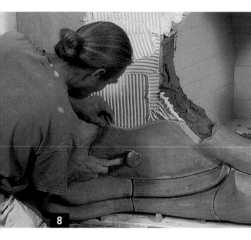

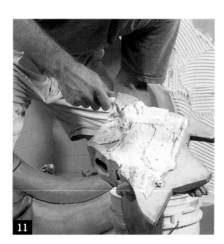

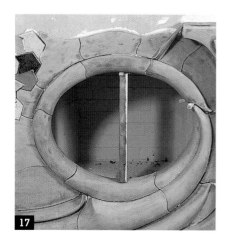

17. Brace the arch with a stick of wood cut to the vertical height of the oval opening.

18. Place the center sections of the mantel and braces, and use a long carpenter's level to shim

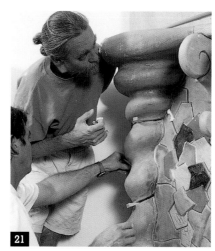

them up (anything that is available for propping up pieces is fair game!).

19. Place the rest of the mantel sections, and add a long strip of duct tape underneath to support the mantel until the mortar sets.

20. Wipe excess thinset off the sections before it sets.

21, 22. Set the capital for the spiral column in place, and further reinforce it with mallet blows.

23. Add more temporary supports underneath sections until you feel that it is secure.

24. Leave the installed work with braces and shims in place until the next day when they can be removed and grout added to the surround.

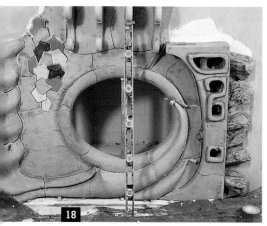

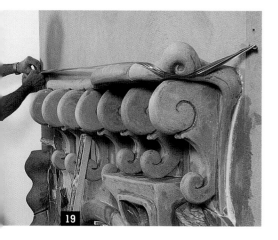

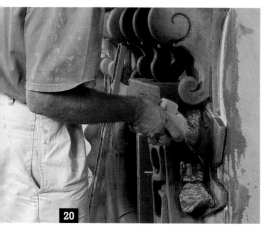

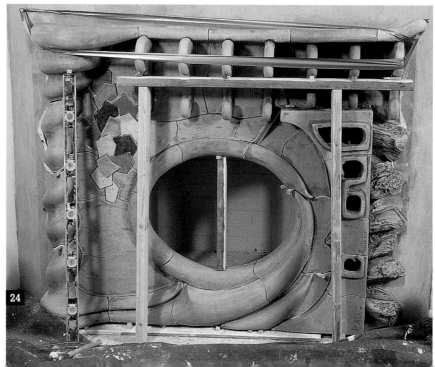

Chapter Six

GALLERY

The following section of works by a variety of architectural ceramicists with differing styles and approaches will amaze and inspire you. You'll see that there are no limits to the concept of architectural ceramics. From public commissions to home installations, the works of all of the artists included in this section have as much to do with form as they do with function.

PETER KING (Pensacola, Florida), *Hogar*, fireplace: 6 ft. 8 in. x 5 ft. 7 in. x 2 ft. 8 in. (2 x 1.6 x 1.4 m), mural: 30 x 96 in. (75 cm x 2.4 m), 1996; glazed and unglazed stoneware; Δ6.

Right: **LIZ SURBECK BIDDLE** (Croton-on-Hudson, New York), *Water Rites,* located at Croton/Harmon Railroad Station, Croton-on-Hudson, New York, 1996; 108 x 96 x 2 in. (2.7 x 2.4 m x 5 cm); tiles, 6 x 6 in. (15 x 15 cm); terra cotta; handmade tiles; Δ04

Below: **ALVING LOVING, JR.** (New York, New York), *Detroit New Morning,* tile mural at Millender Center Station, Detroit People Mover, Detroit, Michigan; design executed by Pewabic Pottery, Detroit; stoneware, press-molded; Δ10. Photo by Balthazar Korab, Ltd.

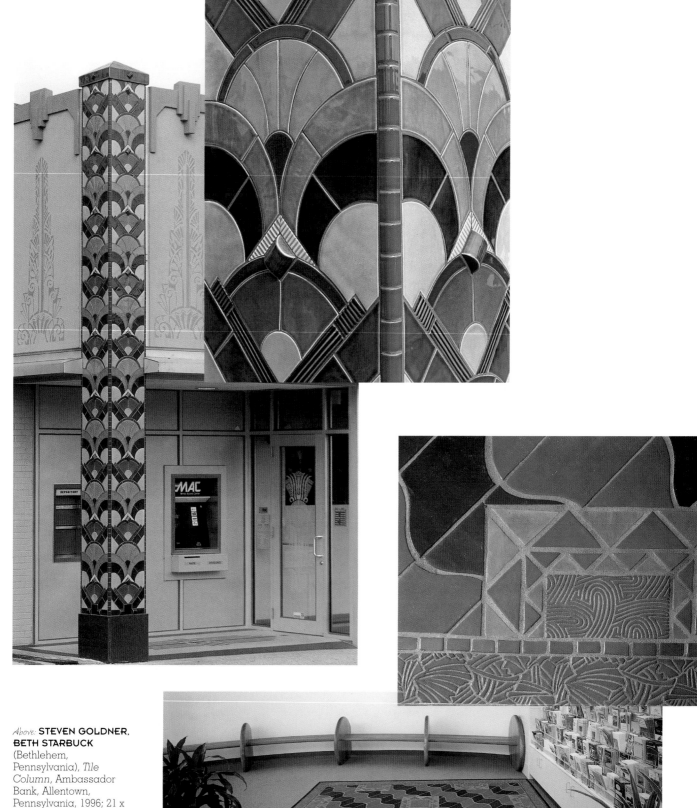

Above: **STEVEN GOLDNER, BETH STARBUCK** (Bethlehem, Pennsylvania), *Tile Column,* Ambassador Bank, Allentown, Pennsylvania, 1996; 21 x 20 x 20 ft. (53 x 50 x 50 cm); stoneware; slab-rolled, molded; Δ6. Photo by Hub Willson

Right: **SUSAN KOWALCZYK** (Rexville, New York), *untitled,* tile floor at North Carolina Welcome Center south of Charlotte, N.C., 1986; 10 ft. x 10 ft. x 3/4 in. (3 m x 3 m x 1.9 cm); earthenware; hand-pressed into molds; Δ03. Photo by David H. Ramsey

Starting at the lower left and continuing clockwise on page 113:

PHYLLIS KUDDER SULLIVAN (Shoreham, New York), *Blue Partita*, 1997-98; 30 x 18 x 12 ft. (9 x 5.4 x 3.6 m); stoneware; woven, extruded coils; Δ6. Photo by J. Sullivan

NICHOLAS WOOD (Arlington, Texas), *A Thousand Nights*, site-specific installation, Saint Paul's Medical Center, Dallas, Texas,1985; 54 x 240 x 6 in. (1.3 x 6 m x 15 cm); terra cotta; extruded coils, hand-rolled and compressed; Δ04-Δ02. Photo by artist

BARBARA SORENSEN (Winter Park, Florida), *Caryatides*, installation at Florida State Capital Complex, Tallahassee, Florida,1998 ; 2 x 10 ft. each (6 x 30 cm); stoneware paper clay; slab-built, wrapped in large coils, embedded stones; Δ6

JUAN GRANADOS (Lubbock, Texas), *First Harvest*, 1994; 18 x 108 x 168 in. (45 cm x 2.7 x 4.2 m); earthenware; hand-formed with slump mold, textured with needle tools; Δ06. Photo by Jon Q. Thompson

Starting at the lower left on page 114 and continuing clockwise on page 115:

PETER KING (Pensacola, Florida), *Etruscan*, fireplace, 9 x 6 ft. (2.7 x 1.8 m); other clay features include molding, sconces, and surrounds; 1989; glazed stoneware, tile pressed and handbuilt; Δ5-6.

DIANA AND TOM WATSON (Hermosa Beach, California), *untitled*, entryway floor, 1997; 120 x 78 in. (3 x 1.9 m); earthenware; hand-molded and ram-pressed tiles; silkscreened pattern, cuerda seca technique; Δ05. Photo by Thomas Watson

F. MICHAEL KING (Escondido, California), *untitled*, 1997; fireplace, 74 x 64 x 8 in. (1.8 x 1.6 m x 20 cm); grog, ball clay, fire clay mixture; glaze removed from carved leaves before firing; Δ5. Photo by artist

PHILIP BELLOMO (Tucson, Arizona), *Moorish Screen*, 1995; 106 x 34 x 1½ in. (265 x 85 x 3.8 cm); porcelain; slip cast from two-piece plaster mold; Δ9. Photo by artist

Starting at the lower left and continuing clockwise:
JEFFREY WARNOCK (Santa Barbara, California), *The Burger-Que,* fuctional barbeque,1995; 44 x 24 x 25 in. (110 x 60 x 62.5 cm); sculpture mix stoneware; slab-built, wheel-thrown, one-piece plaster mold; Δ06. Photo by Phillip Cohen

ELYSE SAPERSTEIN (Elkins Park, Pennsylvania), *Looking for the Light,* wall light,1997; 31 x 6 x 17.5 in. (77.5 x 15 x 43.8 cm); earthenware; slab built; Δ05. Photo by John Carland

PETER KING (Pensacola, Florida), *Pan-da-monium,* bread oven, 8 ft. 6 in. x 6 ft. 6 in. (2.6 x 1.9 m), 1998; glazed stoneware, handbuilt; Δ5-6.

Starting at the lower left and continuing clockwise:

P. MATTSON MCDONALD (Seaview, Washington), *untitled*, upholstered stool, 1997; 18 in. (45 cm) high, 22 in. (55 cm) diameter; stoneware; slip-trailed pattern, wheel-thrown pieces assembled with slip; Δ10. Photo by Bill Bachhuber

SHEL NEYMARK (Embudo, New Mexico), *Blanket Table*, 1997; 30 x 36 x 84 in. (75 x 90 x 210 cm); low-absorption clay; extruded and slab-rolled clay and shards; Δ02. Photo by artist

KREG OWENS (Alexandria, Virginia), *Baptismal Font: Laodicea*, 1998; 46 x 18 x 15 in. (115 x 45 x 37.5 cm); terra cotta; slab-built base with carved, stamped, and sprig embellishments; thrown and altered pedestal and basin with carved, stamped, and sprig additions, pulled handles; Δ04. Photo by artist

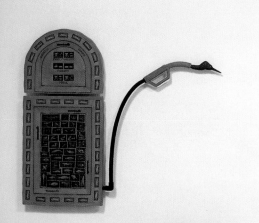

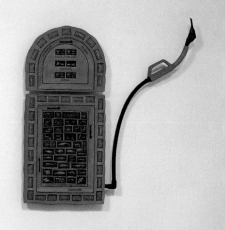

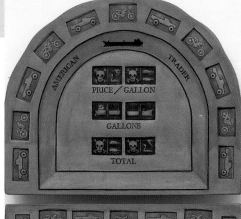

Starting below and continuing clockwise on page 119:

JANE W. LARSON (Bethesda, Maryland), *Chlorophyll Miracle*, embedded water scene,1987; 8 x 13 ft. (2.4 x 3.9 m); white stoneware; local sycamore and hybiscus embedded into clay to create fossil; Δ6. Photo by artist

DAVID K. MORGAN (Miro Loma, California), *American Trader*, 1991; 48 x 180 x 1 in. (1.2 x 4.5 m x 2.5 cm); terra cotta; carved relief with carved wooden blocks; Δ05. Photo by Robert Wedemeyer

MARY LOU ALBERETTI (New Fairfield, Connecticut), *untitled*, bas-relief,1992; 25 x 18 x 4 in. (62.5 x 45 x 10 cm); low-fire earthenware; slab-built, carved and appliqued; Δ06. Photo by artist

KATHRYN STORY (Las Cruces, New Mexico), *A Chunk of the Pond*, gallery installation,1997-98; 10 x 12 x 14 ft. (3 x 3.6 x 4.2 cm); sculpture clay; wall murals: hand-carved; floor: handmade press molded tile, hand-carved; sculptures: coil built and hand-carved; floor: Δ02; wall murals and sculptures: Δ04. Photo by Art Schobey

Starting at the lower left on page 120 and continuing clockwise on page 121:

SUSAN DANNENFEWER AND KIRK BECK (Lafayette, California), *Endangered Frog Fountain,* 1998; 5 x 4½ x 5 ft. (1.5 x 1.3 x 1.5 m); stoneware; hand-sculpted, mold appliqué; Δ5-6. Photo by Dannenbeck Tile

MICHAEL A. FRASCA (Harrodsburg, Kentucky), *Amelia Valerio Weinberg Memorial Fountain,* Hamilton County Public Library, Cincinatti, Ohio,1990; 12 x 14 x 14 ft. (3.6 x 4.2 x 4.2 m); stoneware; hand-pressed in wood and plaster molds, sculpted; Δ7-9

ZOÉ AYN STRECKER (Harrodsburg, Kentucky), *Memorial Fountain,* 1997; 28 x 84 x 84 in. (.7 x 2.1 x 2.1 m); primary form handbuilt, cut into four parts, sculpted and textured; Δ6. Photo by artist

MICHAEL A. FRASCA (Harrodsburg, Kentucky), *untitled,* baptismal fountain and pool, St. Xavier Church, Cincinnati, Ohio, 1994; 3½ x 10 x 10 ft. (1 x 3 x 3 m); stoneware; wood and plaster molds used to hand press and sculpt repeating pieces; Δ09. Photo by Tony Walsh

Starting at the lower left on page 122 and continuing clockwise on page 123:

PETER KING (Pensacola, Florida), *Florida Bar*, 13 ft. 6 in. x 3 ft. 8 in. (4 x 1.1 m),1996; glazed stoneware, handbuilt and slab built; Δ5-6.

LISA BREZNAK (Peekskill, New York), *untitled*, kitchen back-splash,1996; 16 in. x 27 ft. x ½ in. (40 cm x 8.1 m x 1.25 cm); field tile, 5 x 5 in. (12.5 x 12.5 cm); earthenware; slab-built, hand-cut shapes with incised detail; Δ04.
Photo by Howard Goodman

BARBRA KATES (Yelm, Washington), *Egyptian Column*, 1997; 88 x 14 in. (2.2 m x 35 cm); stoneware sculpture body; slab-built, formed over PVC pipe; Δ6. Photo by Mark Frey

MARY KUILEMA (Lowell, Michigan), *Puzzle Fireplace*, 1997; 4 ft. x 4 ft. x ¼ in. (1.2 x 1.2 m x .6 cm); hearth, 66 x 22 x ¼ in. (165 x 55 x .6 cm); stoneware; slab-built, sections bevel-edged and smoothed at leather-hard stage; Δ6. Photo by artist

TERRY NICHOLAS (Ponte Vedra Beach, Florida), *Tile Carpet with Fish*, 1997; 4 x 3 ft. (1.2 x .9 m); earthenware and terra cotta; slab-rolled and cut tiles, hand-set terra-cotta pieces, commercial field tiles; Δ05. Photo by David Porter

Starting at the lower left on page 124 and continuing clockwise on page 125:

JUN KANEKO (Omaha, Nebraska), *untitled*, tile mural at Broadway Station, Detroit People Mover, Detroit Michigan; stoneware; slab-rolled and cut; Δ10. Photo by Balthazar Korab, Ltd.

ALLIE MCGHEE (Detoit, Michigan), *Voyage*, tile mural at Michigan Station, Detroit People Mover, Detroit, Michigan; design executed by Pewabic Pottery, Detroit; earthenware; slab-rolled and hand cut; Δ04. Photo by Balthazar Korab, Ltd.

ELIZABETH GRAJALES (Brooklyn, New York), *A Bird's Life*, detail of tile series, platform in Penn Station, New York City, New York, 1997-98; 12 x 12 x ¼ in. tiles (30 x 30 x 1 cm); stoneware, handmade tile; Δ06. Photo by Orin Slor

TOM PHARDEL (Ann Arbor, Michigan), *In Honor of W. Hawkins Ferry*, tile mural at Times Square Station, Detroit People Mover, Detroit, Michigan; design executed by Pewabic Pottery, Detroit; stoneware; slab-rolled and cut, hand-pressed in molds; Δ10. Photo by Balthazar Korab, Ltd.

Starting at the lower left and continuing clockwise on page 127:

DEBORAH MINTZ (New York, New York), *Mediterranean Melange*, garden sculpture and fountain,1998; 60 x 72 x 5 in. (1.5 x 1.8 m x 12.5 cm); red earthenware; hand-built slab columns, wheel-thrown additions, pressed tiles, extruded tiles, hand-carved tiles; Δ04. Photo by artist

SHEL NEYMARK (Embudo, New Mexico), *Rosalie Doolittle Fountain*, Rio Grande Botanic Garden, Albuquerque, New Mexico, 1994-96; 60 ft. (18 m) plaza; pool, 33 ft. (9.9 m) diameter; bench, 50 x 5 ft. (15 x 1.5 m); heavily grogged and fritted clay; hand-built, hand press molded and ram press molded, slab-rolled and hand-cut, extruded and coiled; Δ02. Overall photo by Herb Lotz. Detail photo by artist.

PETER A. DAVIS (New York, New York) with Evelyn Dow, Lindsey Ann Fink, Bonnie Lee, Mandy Meyers, Kathy Skaggs, *untitled*, mural installation in Samos, Greece, 1998; 38 x 23 x 1 in. (95 x 57.5 x 2.5 cm); earthenware; hand-built, press molded, stamped; Δ04. Photo by Peter A. Davis

PETER KING (Pensacola, Florida), *Annmarie Garden Entry Gates*, each: 15 x 13 x 2½ ft. (4.5 x 3.9 m x 75 cm), 1995; glazed stoneware, handbuilt; Δ5-6.

Starting below and continuing clockwise on page 129:
BETTINA ELSNER (Indian Rocks Beach, Florida), *untitled,* window panels,1995; tiles, 4¾ x 4¾ in. (12 x 12 cm); kaolin; maiolica glaze; Δ05.

NANCI BARNES (Fulton, Texas), *untitled,* door relief, 1997; 23 in. x 7 ft. (57.5 cm x 2.1 m); stoneware; slab and relief sculpture; Δ9. Photo by artist

SUSAN DANNENFEWER AND KIRK BECK (Lafayette, California), *Papyrus Shadow Pool,* 1998; 6 x 10 x 2 ft. (1.8 x 3 m x 60 cm); stoneware; cast column tiles with copper inserts; Δ5-6. Photo by Dannenbeck Tile

SUSAN BEERE (Del Mar, California), *Tropical Fish,* tile entryway,1989; 32 x 32 x 2 in. (80 x 80 x 5 cm); white earthenware; handmade sculpted tile, bas-relief, free-form cut; Δ06. Photo by Hugh L. Wilkerson

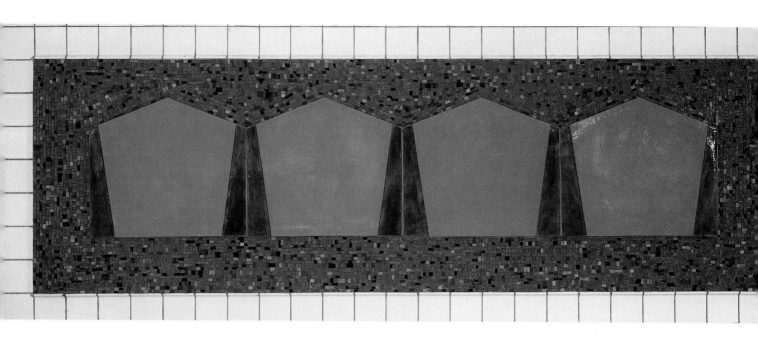

Top to bottom:

FRANK OLT (Oyster Bay Cove, New York), *Temple Quad*, 1992; 36 x 120 x 3 in. (.9 x 3 m x 7.5 cm); stoneware with mosaic glass; wheel-thrown closed forms inverted into press molds; Δ6.
Photo by B. Bunkley

BETH RAVITZ (Coral Springs, Florida), *untitled*, outdoor ceramic wall at Westchester Elmentary School, Coral Springs,1998; 120 x 240 x 8 in. (3 x 6 m x 20 cm); stoneware; hand built with slabs, cracked commercial tile used to form mosaic; Δ06.
Photo by Charlie Freiberg

GEORGE HANDY (Asheville, North Carolina), *Rift Valley*, 1997; 3 x 7 ft. (.9 x 2.1 m); cast tiles, impressed textures, applied slabs; Δ6

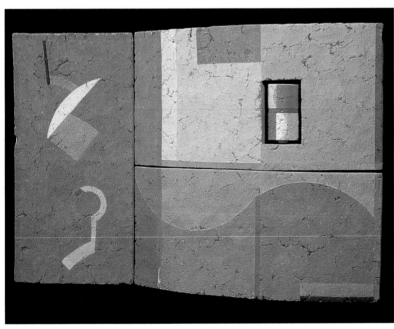

Starting at the lower left and continuing clockwise:
JOSEPH DETWILER (Fredericksburg, Virginia), *Composition with Revolving Inferno*, ceramic relief painting in three parts, 1998; 15 x 22½ x 2 in. (38 x 56 x 5 cm); earthenware, press-molded, cut, rotating cylinder on brass pin; Δ06. Photo by artist

NANCY MCCROSKEY (Fort Wayne, Indiana), *Suite in Black, White, and Grey*, gallery installation, 1995; 60 x 96 x 2 in. (1.5 x 2.4 m x 5 cm); earthenware; slab construction using templates; Δ04

KATHRYN ALLEN (Seattle, Washington), *Wall Fragment*, 1997; 40 x 18 x 3 in. (100 x 45 x 8 cm); stoneware with applied copper, slab-built, individual raku tiles mounted on plywood; Δ09. Photo by T. Holt

Starting at the lower left on page 132 and continuing clockwise on page 133:

ANGELICA POZO (Cleveland, Ohio), *Cleveland: Air Laboratory of the World*, RTA rapid train station, Cleveland Hopkins Airport, 1993; overall: 2000 sq. ft. (180 cm 2), wall panels: 3 ft. x 300 ft. x 8 in. (90 cm x 90 m x 20 cm), floor panels: 2 x 3 ft. (5 x 8 m), 3 x 4 ft. (8 x 10 m), 4 x 4 ft. (10 x 10 m); terra cotta and commercial tile; wall airplanes: coil and slab construction, floor panels: slab-rolled, molded; wall: Δ04, floor: Δ3, Photo by Eric Hanson

KAREN SINGER (Philadelphia, Pennsylvania), *donor wall*, Meriter Foundation, Madison, Wisconsin, 1998; 34 x 111 in. (.8 x 2.7 m); red and white clay; slab-built, low relief sculpting, arches sculpted and cast in plaster; Δ05. Photo by Skot Wiedmann

J. PAUL SIRES (Charlotte, North Carolina), *Drive-By Floral*, mural at Hardee's restaurant in Chapel Hill, North Carolina, 1993; 10 x 5 x 4 ft. (3 x 1.5 x 1.2 m); carved brick; pattern drawn on leather-hard bricks with charcoal, carved at factory; Δ3.

NORMA WALLIS (Baltimore, Maryland), *Octagon Plaza*, tile installation, 1991-94; 25 ft. (7.5 m) diameter; red clay, white stoneware, white stoneware with added iron oxide, white stoneware with added cobalt and chrome oxides; handmade interlocking tiles; Δ02-Δ06. Photo by Joseph Hyde

Starting at the lower left on page 134 and continuing clockwise on page 135:

STEVE HASSLOCK (Covington, Louisiana), *untitled*, gateway to Columbia Street Landing, Covington, Louisiana,1997; 12 x 16 ft. (3.6 x 4.8 m); earthenware; coil and slab-built, high-relief carving; Δ04.
Photo by P. Gould

JOHN DONOVAN (Pensacola, Florida) *Some Lures (For Different Kinds of Fish)*, 1996; 12 ft. long (3.6 m); stoneware, steel, sticks; wheel-thrown, coil-built; Δ06-Δ10.

NORMA WALLIS (Baltimore, Maryland), *Slow Ascent*, wall installation,1997; 34 x 72 x 4 in. (85 x 180 x 10 cm); white earthenware, porcelain; assembled from various works destroyed in 1995 studio fire; handbuilt, carved; Δ6.
Photo by Karcher and Associates

KATHY TRIPLETT (Weaverville, North Carolina), *untitled*, 1997; 7 x 8 x 2 ft. (2.1 x 2.4 m x 60 cm); brown mid-range clay; handbuilt, slab-built, extruded, pinched; Δ04. Photo by artist

LAURIE SPENCER (Tulsa, Oklahoma), *Toad Hall Habitat*, 1990-91; 126 x 120 x 120 in. (3.1 x 3 x 3 m); earthenware; coil-built on site; wood-fired on site in ceramic-fiber kiln; Δ2. Photo by Laurie Spencer

Starting at the lower right on page 136 and continuing clockwise on page 137:

LINDA BLOSSOM (Ithaca, New York), *Window Surround with Egyptian-style Column*, 1994; 71 x 52 x 4 in. (1.7 x 1.3 m x 10 cm); high grog gray stoneware; slab-built; Δ6. Photo by Andy Gillis

TOM LANE (St. Paul, Minnesota), *untitled*, column panels, 1997, 22 x 24 x 3 in. (55 x 60 x 7.5 cm); stoneware; model for mold made from extruded shapes; Δ10. Photo by artist

RENEÉ O'CONNOR (Ocean Park, Washington), *Ginkgo Fireplace Columns and Wall*, 1997, 66 x 60 x 8 in. (1.6 x 1.5 m x 20 cm); stoneware; molded relief tiles, slab-rolled field tiles, extruded trim; Δ6. Photo by Courtney Frisse

NAWAL AND KARIM MOTAWI (Ann Arbor, Michigan), *untitled*, 1995; 4 x 50 x 90 in. (10 cm x 1.2 x 2.2 m); porcelain; tiles pressed with hydraulic press; Δ9. Photo by Nawal Motawi

ALICE TURNER (Clearlake Shores, Texas), *untitled*, mosaic tile threshold, 1995; 53½ x 18½ x ⅝ in. (133.8 x 46.3 x 1.6 cm); earthenware; tiles cut from slab; Δ06. Photo by Debra Rueb

RICHARD AERNI, MICHAEL FRASCA, ALLEN NAIRN (Harrodsburg, Kentucky), *untitled*, niche relief at Omni Netherland Plaza Hotel, Cincinnati, Ohio, 1985; 12 x 12 x 3 ft. (3.6 x 3.6 x .9 m); talc clay body; slip-cast border, hand-built tiles; Δ04. Photo by Allen Nairn

Starting at the lower left on page 138 and continuing clockwise on page 139:

ISAIAH ZAGAR (Philadephia, Pennsylvania), *Church of Crucifixion,* outside wall, 1995; 12 x 25 ft. (3.6 x 7.5 m); hand-painted tiles, mirrors, ceramic shards, found objects.
Photo by Barry Halkin

TOBY MARTIN, DONNA PICKENS, MARIANNE WEINBERG-BENSON (Atlanta, Georgia), *The Tower of Time and The Community Quilt,* collaborative piece located at Ben Hill Recreation Center, Atlanta, Georgia, 1997; tower, 264 x 84 x 84 in. (6.6 x 2.1 x 2.1 m); quilts, 120 x 144 x 2 in. (3 x 3.6 m x 5 cm); hand-carved bricks fired commercially.
Photo by Weinberg-Benson

ED AND CORNELIA GATES (Corpus Cristi, Texas), *Paseo de la Flor at the Selena Memorial,* Corpus Cristi, Texas, 1997; 84 x 480 x ⅜ in. (flat tile) or ½ in. (relief tile) (2.1 m x 12 m x .9 cm or 1.3 cm); red stoneware; slab-built flat tiles, press-molded relief tiles; Δ6. Photo by Ed Gates

CHRISTY HENGST (Sante Fe, New Mexico), *untitled,* bus stop, Santa Fe Community College, 1995; 12 x 10 x 6 ft. (3.6 x 3 x 1.8 m); stoneware; handmade carved and uncarved tiles; Δ10. Photo by artist

GLOSSARY

"Back butter". An expression used to describe adding a thick application of mortar to the back of sections of ceramics before applying them to the substrate.

Bat. A plaster, wood, or plastic disc which ceramicists use to transport pottery around the studio and to the kiln.

Bisque. A preliminary firing of ware which removes all moisture from the piece and provides a more stable form with which to work when applying decorations and glazes.

Bone dry. The stage of clay dryness at which the clay has been air-dried until it is as dry as possible prior to firing.

Box building. The construction of geometric, hollow clay forms, such as columns, out of slabs that are supported by internal bracing.

Brayer. A small ink roller that can be used for smoothing clay.

Candle period. A long period of slow firing.

Cowling. A hood added to the front of a fireplace to vent heat.

Chuck. An open container, or doughnut of soft clay with a hole in the center, that is used to hold a clay form, such as a sink, in place for trimming on the wheel or for drying.

Clay body. A mixture of natural clay and other structurally compatible materials that make the clay workable and ideal for firing at certain temperatures. Clay bodies suited for architectural ceramics usually contain a high percentage of coarse material, or grog, which leaves spaces in the clay that allow moisture to escape.

Die. A form made of plastic or wood in a particular shape that is used for cutting or extruding clay.

Drape (hump) mold. A support, such as a plaster mold or wooden frame, in or over which a clay slab is draped in order to shape it while it stiffens.

Draw tool. A type of die that is used for shaping clay into various profiles. The profile is transferred to the clay by repeatedly pulling the tool over the clay.

Extruder. A tool used for forming moist clay that contains a steel, plastic, wood, or ceramic die at the end of a hollow steel chamber through which the clay is pressed.

Firebricks. Bricks made especially to handle heat load that make convenient, inexpensive, and durable kiln stilts for architectural pieces.

Freeze thaw spalling. A flaking effect on the surface of ceramic pieces installed outdoors caused by exposure to freezing conditions.

Glaze. A substance composed primarily of silica that creates a glassy coating that is fused onto the surface of the clay when fired. Glazes may be matte or glossy, depending on their components.

Grog. Fired clay particles with larger sizes which serve to "open" a clay body and therefore reduce shrinkage, cracking, and warping. Grog also helps the clay body to dry.

Leather hard. The stage of clay dryness at which the clay is dry enough to retain fingermarks, but still wet enough to be carved or joined. At this stage, much of the moisture has evaporated and shrinkage has just ended.

Maquette. A scaled-down model of a piece of sculpture or architectural ceramics used to make decisions before constructing the larger piece.

Outrigger. An extension, such as a wooden board, that is clamped to a table to extend the dimensions of a work surface for laying foundation slabs.

Overspray. Glaze droplets which float in the air during the glazing process that can be hazardous to breathe. The use of a high volume, low pressure (HVLP) sprag gun reduces overspray.

Point load. The weight of large pieces should be distributed over the surface of the shelf so that the *point load,* or amount of downward force, is distributed across the shelf.

Pug mill. A machine used to blend clay into a workable consistency, recycle clay scraps, remove air from moist clay, and extrude round pugs of usable clay.

Pyrometer. An instrument used to measure the exact internal temperature of a kiln during firing and cooling in order to monitor the rate of firing.

"Sew". To join the walls of two slabs together by dragging a needle tool embedded in the soft clay back and forth across the joining seam. The term "sew" was adapted by Peter King to describe this particular type of deep clay scoring.

METRIC CONVERSIONS

Shuttle (car) kiln. A large kiln that has shelves that slide out on a support. Because of the size of architectural pieces, shuttle kilns are ideal for firing architectural ceramic work.

Shrinkage rate. The rate at which clay shrinks after firing. This percentage is added to the desired final dimensions of an architectural piece when building the piece in clay so that, after firing and shrinking, the piece will conform to the actual dimensions.

Substrate. In architectural ceramics, this term indicates the underlying surface, such as brick, drywall, or plywood, onto which ceramic sections are attached. Substrates require various materials for proper installation.

Slab roller. A mechanical roller that produces clay slabs of even thickness that are used to lay the foundation of and build architectural pieces. This tool is as important to studio architectural work as a potter's wheel is to most studio potteries.

Sprigging. A type of ceramic relief decoration made by attaching molded clay to damp clay surfaces. Molds for this type of applied decoration can be made by making plaster castings of found objects or building a relief in moist clay and casting it. Sprigging can be applied as decoration by scoring the section and the area to which it is to be applied, brushing on a small amount of slip, and then joining the section to the surface.

Wet dimensions. The dimensions of wet clay with shrinkage added.

Inches	Cm	Inches	Cm
⅛	0.3	20	50.8
¼	0.6	21	53.3
⅜	1.0	22	55.9
½	1.3	23	58.4
⅝	1.6	24	61.0
¾	1.9	25	63.5
⅞	2.2	26	66.0
1	2.5	27	68.6
1¼	3.2	28	71.1
1½	3.8	29	73.7
1¾	4.4	30	76.2
2	5.1	31	78.7
2½	6.4	32	81.3
3	7.6	33	83.8
3½	8.9	34	86.4
4	10.2	35	88.9
4½	11.4	36	91.4
5	12.7	37	94.0
6	15.2	38	96.5
7	17.8	39	99.1
8	20.3	40	101.6
9	22.9	41	104.1
10	25.4	42	106.7
11	27.9	43	109.2
12	30.5	44	111.8
13	33.0	45	114.3
14	35.6	46	116.8
15	38.1	47	119.4
16	40.6	48	121.9
17	43.2	49	124.5
18	45.7	50	127.0
19	48.3		

Volumes

1 fluid ounce	29.6 ml
1 pint	473 ml
1 quart	946 ml
1 gallon (128 fl. oz.)	3.785 l

Weights

0.035 ounces	1 gram
1 ounce	28.35 grams
1 pound	453.6 grams

Temperatures

To convert fahrenheit to centigrade (Celsius), subtract 32, multiply by 5, and divide by 9.

To convert centigrade (Celsius) to fahrenheit, multiply by 9, divide by 5, and add 32.

Contributing Artists

The following artists' works are shown on the pages listed after their names:

Peter King (Pensacola, FL), cover, title page, 6, 7, 11, 12, 34, 49, 63, 77, 78, 91, 94, 109, 115, 116, 122, 127, back cover

Richare Aerni, Michael Frasca, and **Allen Nairn** (Harrodsburg, KY), 137

Mary Lou Alberetti (New Fairfield, CT), 119

Kathryn Allen (Seattle, WA), 76, 131

Nanci Barnes (Fulton, TX), 128

Susan Beere (Del Mar, CA), 129

Philip Bellomo (Tucson, AZ), 115

Liz Surbeck Biddle (Croton-on-Hudson, NY), 110

Linda Blossom (Ithaca, NY), 136

Liza Breznak (Peekskill, NY), 93,122

Susan Dannenfewer and **Kirk Beck** (Lafayette, CA), 120, 129

Lee Davis (Brasstown, NC), 48

Mary Kay Davis (Baton Rouge, LA), 49

Peter A. Davis (New York, NY), 127

Joseph Detwiler (Fredericksburg, VA), 131

John Donovan (Pensacola, FL), 134

Jan Edwards (Portland, OR), 91

Bettina Elsner (Indian Rocks Beach, FL), 128

Michael A. Frasca (Harrodsburg, KY), 11, 120

Ed and **Cornelia Gates** (Corpus Cristi, TX), 139

Steven Goldner and **Beth Starbuck** (Bethlehem, PA), 111

Elizabeth Grajales (Brooklyn, NY), 125

Juan Granados (Lubbock, TX), 113

George Handy (Asheville, NC), 130

Robert Harrison (Helena, MT), 10

Steve Hasslock (Covington, LA), 135

Chrity Hengst (Sante Fe, NM), 139

Juan Kaneko (Omaha, NE), 124

Barbara Kates (Yelm, WA), 123

F. Michael King (Escondido, CA), 115

Susan Kowalczyk (Rexville, NY), 111

Mary Kuilema (Lowell, MI), 123

Tom Lane (St. Paul, MN), 136

Jane W. Larson (Bethesda, MD), 118

Alving Loving, Jr. (New York, NY), 110

Xinia Marin (San Jose, Costa Rica), 64

Toby Martin, Donna Pickens, and **Marianne Weinberg-Benson** (Atlanta, GA), 138

Nancy McCroskey (Fort Wayne, IN), 131

P. Mattson McDonald (Seaview, WA), 117

Allie McGhee (Detroit, MI), 125

Deborah Mintz (New York, NY), 126

David K. Morgan (Miro Loma, CA), 118

Nawal and **Karim Motawi** (Ann Arbor, MI), 136

Shel Neymark (Embudo, NM), 117, 126, back cover

Terry Nicholas (Ponte Vedra Beach, FL), 93, 123

Reneé O'Conner (Ocean Park, WA), 136

Frank Olt (Oyster Bay Cove, NY), 130

Kreg Owens (Alexandria, VA), 117

Carrie Anne Parks (Riverdale, MI), 22

Tom Phardel (Ann Arbor, MI), 125

Angela Pozo (Cleveland, OH), 77, 132

Beth Ravitz (Coral Springs, FL), 130

Elyse Saperstein (Elkins Park, PA), 116

Karen Singer (Philadelphia, PA), 132

J. Paul Sires (Charlotte, NC), 8, 133

Barbara Sorensen (Winter Park, FL), 112, back cover

Laurie Spencer (Tusa, OK), 135

Kathryn Story (Las Cruces, NM), 118

Zoé Ayn Strecker (Harrodsburg, KY), 121

Phyllis Kudder Sullivan (Shoreham, NY), 112

Michael Thornton (Albuquerque, NM), 11

John Toki (Richmond, CA), 11, 40

Kathy Triplett (Weaverville, NC), 49, 135

Alice Turner (Clearlake Shores, TX), 137

Norma Wallis (Baltimore, MD), 133, 135

Jeffrey Warnock (Santa Barbara, CA), 116

Diana and **Tom Watson** (Hermosa Beach, CA), 77, 114

Nicholas Wood (Arlington, TX), 112

W. Mitch Yung (Branson, MO), 92

Isaiah Zagar (Philadelphia, PA), 138

RECOMMENDED READING

Barnard, Julian. *Victorian Ceramic Tiles*. Greenwich, Connecticut: New York Graphic Society, 1972.

Bitters, Stan. *Environmental Ceramics*. New York: Van Nostrand Reinhold Co., 1976.

Byrne, Michael. *Setting Ceramic Tile*. Newtown, Connecticut: Taunton Press, 1987.

Cardew, Michael. *Pioneer Pottery*. New York: St. Martin's Press, 1971.

Giorgini, Frank. *Handmade Tiles*. Asheville, North Carolina: Lark Books, 1994.

Hamilton, David. *The Thames and Hudson Manual of Architectural Ceramics*. London: Thames and Hudson, 1978.

Khalili, Nader. *Ceramic Houses and Earth Architecture: How to Build Your Own*. Los Angeles: Burning Gate Press, 1990.

Kinkead, Cookie. *Fireplaces*. San Francisco: Chronicle Books, 1992.

Kostof, Spiro. *A History of Architecture, Settings and Rituals*. New York: Oxford University Press, 1995.

Kurutz, Gary F. *The Architectural Terra Cotta of Gladding, McBean*. Sausilito, California: Wingate Press, 1989.

Lemmen, Hans van. *Tiles: 1,000 Years of Architectural Decoration*. New York: Abrams, 1993.

Lucie-Smith, Edward. *The Story of Craft*. New York: Van Nostrand Reinhold, 1984.

Furniture: A Concise History. New York: Oxford University Press, 1979.

Michels, Caroll. *How to Survive and Prosper as an Artist*. New York: Holt, Rhinehart, and Winston, 1983.

Miller, Charles. *Tips and Techniques for Builders*. Newtown, Connecticut: Taunton Press, 1988.

Petrie, W. M. Flinders. *Decorative Symbols and Motifs for Artists and Craftspeople*. New York: Dover Publications, 1986.

Reed, Cleota. *Henry Chapman Mercer and the Moravian Pottery and Tileworks*. Philadelphia: University of Pennsylvania Press, 1987.

Rigau, Jorge. *Puerto Rico 1900: Turn of the Century Architecture in the Hispanic Caribean, 1890-1930*. New York: Rizzoli, 1992.

Rindge, Ronald L. Y. and Thomas W. Doyle. *Ceramic Art of the Malibu Potteries, 1926-1932*. Malibu, California: Malibu Lagoon Museum, 1988.

Salvadori, Mario George. *The Art of Construction*. Chicago: Chicago Review Press, 1990.

Self, Charles R. *Joinery: Methods of Fastening Wood*. Pownal, Vermont: Storey Communications, 1991.

Stratton, Michael. *The Terracotta Revival*. London: Victor Gollancz in association with Peter Crawley, 1993.

ACKNOWLEDGMENTS

Thanks

To Mark Price, Steve Hayworth, and John Yanger for setting me on this path so many years ago.

To Barry Coker and Mike Jones for letting me put handmade tiles and sinks in the homes they were building back in '75.

To Kathryn Allen, Nancy Hayes, and Marni Jamie, who pushed me forward in many ways.

To my best friend, Dr. Dennis Golladay, an educator who convinced me I could educate and write a book.

To my best friend, Bernard Pennington, a psychotherapist who convinced me it was okay to be crazy.

To Katherine Duncan, my editor, who put up with my stubborn intellect throughout the editorial process.

To Evan Bracken, without whose photos the book would not stand.

To Kathy Holmes, whose good humor carried us through a very long photo shoot, and whose keen eye has made another beautiful book.

To Nancy Lauck Solono, whose assistance and direction brought the book together.

XINIA MARIN (San Jose, Costa Rica), *Aguada La Florida*, 40 x 32 in. (100 x 80 cm); stoneware; ∆6.

To all those who have worked at Stonehaus over the years: Tiffany Sherman, Corbin McMullin, Jason Stokes, Nevin Macathan, Corina St. Martin, and, particularly, Rob Hayes.

To John Donovan, who went from being my student to my employee to becoming an important teacher and an inspiration now, when, after all these years, I need to start anew.

To all my friends in Costa Rica where this book was written: Carlos y Blanca, Manuel y Carmen, Sergio y Ruth, Professors Ivette Guier and Xinia Marin, and all the students of the Taller de Ceramica of the University of Costa Rica.

To Gary Langhammer, who took such luscious photos of my finished work, and whose installation photos made the projects chapter complete.

And special thanks

To Linda Blossom, who nudged me to begin writing this book in 1991, then patiently helped to organize what I've learned over the past 28 years and assemble it on the written page.

To my brother, John King, a master craftsman who has been my right arm for the past 17 years, and who was instrumental in the development of many of the techniques that you'll find within these covers.

To Xinia Marin for her contribution to the book, my education in ceramics, and my life.

To all the artists who contributed images for this book, and also to those whose works couldn't be included. There was just too much good work. Keep on creating.

INDEX